The Book of Many Flames

Everyday Alchemy
With Esoteric Energies

Angela Orora Medway-Smith

Copyright © Angela Orora Medway-Smith 2022

www.cariadspiritual.com

All rights reserved.

This book is sold subject to the condition that it shall not, by way of trade or otherwise, be hired out, lent or resold, or otherwise circulated without the author's/publisher's prior consent in any form of binding or cover other than that in which it is published and without a similar condition including this condition being imposed on the subsequent publisher.

The moral rights of the author have been asserted.

Disclaimer: This book is designed for educational purposes only. This is not a substitute for, nor does it replace professional training, professional medical advice, diagnosis, or treatment. If you have any concerns or questions about your health, you should always consult with a healthcare professional. The use of any information provided in this book is solely at your own risk.

Dedication

This book is dedicated to my beautiful children. I am so grateful that you have chosen me as your mother on this life's journey. My love for you is without bounds.

Contents

"Power Awaits You!" 1
Preface 2
Introduction 6

Part One: Before You Begin 8
Spiritual Awakening 9
Awakening & Ascension Symptoms 10
Self-Love & Self-Care 12
Preparation 13
Spiritual Protection 13
Managing your Energy 15
Journaling 15
Energetic Tools & Techniques 16
Prayer, Invocation, Ritual and Affirmation 17
Past Life Recall 18
Gratitude & Grounding 18

Part Two: What It's All About 20
What Are the Sacred Flames and Divine Rays? 21
Who Are The Patrons of The Divine Rays? 22
How To Choose Which Sacred Flame To Invoke 23

Channelling Healing Energy For Others 23

Distant, Absent and Hands-On Healing 27

How To Invoke the Sacred Flames 28

The Process 31

Relax And Energetically Clear Yourself 31

Ground 34

Call In Your Guides and Guardians 34

Visualise The Sacred Symbol 34

Invoke The Sacred Flame 34

Intend The Energy And Allow It To Flow Where Intended 35

Cease The Flow And Disconnect Your Energy 35

Give Thanks to the Patrons, Guides And Guardians 35

Feedback And Record-Keeping 36

Anchoring The Light Of The Sacred Flames 36

Part Three: The Sacred Flames & The Divine Rays 38

The Magdalene Flame 151

The Threefold or Ascension Flame 155

Part Four: Seeking Support & Activating Allies 158

Support From Guides and Guardians 159

Allies From The Plant Kingdom 160

Vibrational Healing 161

Plants As Food 163

Plants As Medicine 164

Australian Bush Flower Essences 164

Ayurveda 164

Bach Flower Remedies 165

Essential Oils 166

Flower Essences, Waters and Extracts 166

Herbal Medicine 168

Homeopathy 168

Naturopathy 169

Nutritional Therapy 170

Traditional Chinese Medicine 170

Plants Supporting Spiritual Development 171

Herbs/Resins 171

Sacred Oils 172

The Sacred Flames Alphabetically by Divine Ray 174

A Final Message from the Patrons of the Divine Rays 178

Thank You! 179

Bibliography 180

Glossary 181

Other Work by Angela Orora 184

About the Author 186

"Power Awaits You!"

"Beloveds, there is a need for individuals, for groups, to begin to employ the Sacred Flames. Their energy will support All that there is.

Their power, their capacity to bring healing and change is unsurpassed.

They are the fires of the Divine, each representing a unique aspect of creation; you would do well, dearest one, to engage with them and invoke their power for the highest good of all.

These pages will invite you to become acquainted with the Sacred Fires, their Patrons and their unique individual power.

Be aware of the effect on your own energy body, your spirit, your soul and your ascension path; as always, the choice is yours.

Choose wisely, beloveds. Welcome to the beginning of a new part of this human life!

The Ascended Master St Germain
Channelled by Angela Orora, January 2022

Preface

This book follows *The Book of Many Colours: Awaken Your Soul's Purpose With The Divine Rays,* which introduces the incredible range of divine energies that humanity has had access to since 2012 and the personal and spiritual development that can occur when you tap into them.

The Book of Many Flames is a natural extension, deepening your understanding of the active principles, the driving force of the Divine Rays, the Esoteric or Sacred Flames and introducing you to their use as a source of healing energy, knowledge and inspiration for the self, others and All that there is.

Both are designed as practical handbooks, jumping-off points of discovery in what I hope for you will be the beginning of a relationship with some of the most highly evolved beings in our Universe.

This book brings practical guidance on how to employ the Esoteric Fires of the Divine Rays to bring alchemical transformation and healing for the highest good of all.

The Patrons want YOU to connect with them and use these resources. They want to support you, bring you knowledge, share their wisdom and guide you in the use of the Esoteric Flames. You have been drawn to this book for a reason. Your Soul is seeking to grow and YOU have been chosen to be a bringer of change.

Wherever you are on your journey of spiritual discovery, please don't skip the **Before You Begin** section. It contains important information for your safety, comfort and protection.

First, let me share with you how these books and the ones that will follow have come about.

I began channelling the Ascended Master St Germain in 2018 when he became a regular visitor to the spiritual development classes I was teaching. The more I channelled, the clearer my connection to the Ascended Master and Angelic Collectives became. I was learning to allow my consciousness to lean aside and allow my physical body to be used as a tool for these beings of light to communicate with mankind.

My 'training' continued and I was led to people who could support me with this work. Instruction and messages about the books I channel to support you, dear reader, flow clearly.

Each book has a purpose, which is to awaken divine souls like you and allow you to explore your own abilities, supporting you on your spiritual and human journeys on this beautiful planet.

Looking back, every choice I have made, every job I have held has prepared me and brought me to where I am today. My soul's purpose is to awaken, empower, enable, inspire and support people on their own journey of healing and spiritual discovery, and to transform their lives and help them soar to their soul's highest potential.

The Ascended Masters St Germain and Lord Lanto, in particular, are very keen that this information reaches more people, that more beautiful souls are empowered and enlightened by accessing the Divine Rays and their Esoteric Flames using simple, practical techniques.

In fact, the Divine Rays and their Esoteric Fires have been accessible to mankind since the time of Lemuria. In our recent history, this information has been kept hidden, and even when the great channels Madame Blavatsky, Guy Ballard and Alice Bailey made this information available, it was still inaccessible to most.

So, here it is, another practical handbook to help you access and enjoy communion with the Divine Rays, this time going deeper and working with their active principles, the Esoteric Fires.

I hope that you will find between these pages a source of healing, knowledge, peace, joy and increased wisdom to support you on your life's journey.

I feel truly blessed that the Ascended Masters have chosen me, amongst many other lightworkers, as their mouthpiece. I hope you enjoy their words, find comfort, strength and inspiration on these pages and are subsequently able to translate your intention into action for the benefit of ALL.

Brightest and abundant blessings,

Angela Orora Medway-Smith

"Great spirits have always encountered violent opposition from mediocre minds."

Albert Einstein

Introduction

This book builds from *The Book of Many Colours: Awaken Your Soul's Purpose With The Divine Rays*. In its introduction I explain that everything, 'ALL that there is', you, the chair you sit on, our beloved planet is simply made of atoms and molecules that vibrate at different rates.

That, the light, sound, and energy vibrations - such as the different frequency waves which carry data that floods our planet - are equally made up of different vibrations.

I go on to explain about the Divine Rays, the primary vibrational essences of our Universe, each of which holds a unique frequency. I introduce you to their Patrons (Ascended Masters sometimes known as The Great White Brotherhood), Cosmic Ascended Masters, Archangels, and Angelic Collectives, sacred symbols, practical applications, aligning crystalline energy and I include channelled messages and affirmations from the Patrons themselves.

The Patrons now feel that YOU are ready to harness the power of the esoteric energies that fuel the Divine Rays; the Esoteric or Sacred Flames.

Within these pages, you will find information and instruction on how to connect with these sacred energies and how you can use their alchemical energy for the benefit of self, others and All that there is.

Also contained are my channellings from the Patrons with their specific guidance on the use of the Sacred Flames. You will notice as you work through them that YOU are encouraged to follow your intuition in their use, the Patrons are keen that this is your starting point, that you employ choice on your path using the Sacred Flames. I would also encourage you to follow your intuition, your inner truth, on how you choose to connect with and utilise these energies, always doing so with an open heart and mind.

My wish is that you find inspiration, guidance and the practical tools that will enable you to bring support and healing to All that there is within these pages.

The Sacred Flames are tremendously powerful esoteric energies. Do not underestimate their capacity, dear reader.

Prepare yourself for an enormous personal energetic shift when you engage with them, follow your intuition and remember what Albert Einstein said!

Part One

Before You Begin

"There is but one cause of human failure and that is man's lack of faith in his true Self."

William James

Spiritual Awakening

The concept of the spiritual awakening has been around for centuries and can be seen in a variety of cultures and religions around the world.

Some call it *nirvana*; others call it *enlightenment* or *bliss*. A spiritual awakening begins the moment a person can step back and wake up to their life with a new sense of being in this world.

The idea of spiritual awakening was popularized in the Western world by psychiatrist Carl Jung (who described the process as coming back to the original self), but the experience of rising to a higher state of consciousness has always been an intrinsic part of what it means to be human.

A spiritual awakening can be triggered by any event, from the mundane to the completely life-altering. For many people, a spiritual awakening can be unnerving as you begin to look beyond everyday life and see the enormous possibilities and the never-ending questions. There is so much information available today it can be very confusing; thousands of so-called experts tell you that theirs is the correct path.

If you are reading this book, the chances are that you have already encountered a spiritual awakening, and your thirst for knowledge has brought you to seek information, answers and opportunities for development.

Please remember that every person, every spiritual teacher, has their own perspective and it is up to you to find and walk on your own path. It is important to exercise discernment, follow your intuition and ultimately to find your own truth.

It has always been my experience that when I am ready a teacher appears to guide me; sometimes the lessons I have learned have been difficult, sometimes joyful, but always valuable.

Learning to discern, to truly follow your intuition, is a key skill in life and I wish you clarity on your journey.

> *The Art Of Knowing, Is Knowing What to Ignore.*
>
> Rumi

Awakening & Ascension Symptoms

A spiritual awakening can often feel like opening the door to a new life, as changes and shifts in your perception, psychological changes, physical changes or energetic shifts occur that make you feel completely different.

It might help you to understand that you are not alone and that these changes are perfectly normal.

Here are some signs that you have 'awakened' or are going through a spiritual awakening and becoming tuned into All that there is:

- You have a general feeling of disconnection from everyday life
- You re-examine and re-evaluate long-held beliefs
- Your dreams become more vivid and you may experience sleep disturbance
- You experience more synchronicities and déjà vu
- Relationships with friends and loved ones begin to shift and change
- You feel spirituality becoming an important part of your life
- You become more intuitive and have a keener sense of inauthenticity and manipulation
- You may have experienced a very rough patch, sometimes called the 'dark night of the soul'
- You realize everyone is on their own path

- ❀ You may want to be of service
- ❀ Your teachers appear
- ❀ You feel more connected to the natural world and realise that we are all one
- ❀ You become more sensitive to physical and energetic stimuli
- ❀ You feel a need to change old habits and routines
- ❀ You change your diet
- ❀ Your outlook on the world feels different
- ❀ You feel increased empathy and display more compassion
- ❀ You have a newfound childlike curiosity

All of these feelings are very common.

This is a very exciting time to be alive!

There are huge shifts happening, not simply for individuals but for the planet herself. This process is called 'Ascension' by those in the spiritual community and what you have been experiencing may have been what are known as Ascension Symptoms.

Ascension is a huge subject and there are many very different views held by different spiritual teachers. The best book I have found is *Ascension to Go* by Edwin Courtenay, which gives a very thorough examination of the subject and a suggested further reading list.

My wish for you is:

As You Start To Walk On The Way, The Way Appears.

Rumi

Self-Love & Self-Care

When you go through any major changes in your life, it's important to nurture yourself; otherwise, it can feel a little bit like constantly riding a rollercoaster.

When you are new to working with energy and beings of light, there is a need to practice self-love and self-compassion; be kind to yourself and trust the unfolding will happen in divine timing.

Spiritual development is not a race. Whilst it may feel exciting to absorb every new piece of information and have a go at every new practice, it is wise to take your time.

Your spiritual energy is being brought back into balance with your true self, and therefore, you need to pay attention to your intuition, your inner guide and your inner truth.

You may like to adopt some simple daily self-care rituals, a daily spiritual protection practice, learn to calm your 'monkey mind' and your inner critic.

Remember that you have been programmed by parents, teachers, and society with a set of beliefs that may no longer feel right to you. Your spiritual reset takes time, patience and often resilience.

I feel it's incredibly helpful to practice self-healing and there are many beautiful energy healing modalities which you can choose from that can support your physical and energetic well-being (Lord Lanto has asked me to mention Divine Energy Healing here!).

Above all, listen to your body; it is the physical vehicle for your spirit while you walk this earthly path. You cannot follow your soul's path without it!

Preparation

Much of the introductory material in this section is repeated from *The Book of Many Colours*. If you haven't already read it and absorbed the messages, then please continue reading. If you have, it may still be worth skimming over the pages as a reminder of the preparation needed before embarking on spiritual work and practices that can support your ongoing spiritual development.

Spiritual Protection

Would you leave your front door wide open while you are asleep? Would you walk out in a storm without a coat?

Similarly, it is just not sensible to begin any spiritual practice without considering protection. Spiritual or psychic protection is an essential first step before opening the door to the spirit world or beginning any spiritual practice.

It was the first thing I was taught as a complete novice, and it is the first thing I teach my students, quite simply to prevent attracting any negative energy.

Spiritual protection is not complicated; it simply involves requesting protection from higher powers before you begin any spiritual work. In fact, I don't start my day or get out of bed without calling in my guides and Guardian Angel.

There are hundreds and hundreds of prayers, rituals, or invocations you can choose from, or you could use visualisation instead. In my experience, a personal prayer can be very powerful, so I would encourage you to write your own.

However, here is a simple prayer or invocation you can use if you prefer:

Simple Daily Protection

Divine Spirit, Creator of All,

I call forth now my guides and ministering angels,

To draw close, to bring me guidance and protection,

Now, and until I leave this earthly realm

Amen (or any ending you prefer)

Here is a simple visualisation that you can use to protect your space and yourself before you start a spiritual practice:

Divine Protection Visualisation

- Visualise a pinpoint of divine energy from the Creator in the centre of the room in front of you.
- Begin to expand this point of energy until it grows to the size of a golf ball, an orange, a football, a beach ball, and increase the size of this sphere of divine light until it completely encircles you.
- It then fills the room you are in, reaching into every corner.
- It fills your home and expands further until it reaches out into every corner of your garden, into the street.
- On the outside of this sphere of divine light, place the colour platinum to repel negativity.
- This platinum layer can be as light as gossamer silk or as heavy as a coat of platinum paint on days you feel a bit more vulnerable.

On days where you may feel vulnerable (we all have these), you can layer up your spiritual protection with prayer, visualisation and also by carrying crystals that have a protective energy. On the whole, the Law of Attraction ensures that we attract what we put out into the Universe.

If you think negative thoughts, you attract negative energy and experiences, so it follows that if you think positive thoughts, you attract the positive. (If you do want to delve deeper into psychic protection, there is a fabulous book by Caitlin Matthews, *The Psychic Protection Handbook: Powerful protection for Uncertain Times*.)

Managing Your Energy

We are all unique beings. We all vibrate at different rates. We all have a different capacity for channelling spiritual energy, and it is really important that you are aware of the effect of these different vibrations on your physical and energetic body. Learn to listen to your body and how it responds to different frequencies.

Special care is needed by those of you with diabetes. You will notice that channelling spiritual energy draws on your reserves, so please be careful. Even with almost forty years of experience channelling different spiritual energies, I sometimes still get caught out!

Journaling

Keeping a journal is a really helpful practice. That way, you can track your progress and express your gratitude for the energies as you begin to work with the Divine Rays and Sacred Flames, checking in with yourself on a regular basis, seeing how you are developing, how your life is changing. You can decide on what you want to record and how you measure the changes.

For a free downloadable spiritual journal to record your experiences with the Sacred Flames, go to my website https://www.cariadspiritual.com/sacredflames

Energetic Tools & Techniques

I'd like to talk here about visualisation, crystals, colours, symbols, sigils and sacred geometry. These are all enormous subjects, and you will find thousands of books, huge encyclopaedias, and literally tons of information on the internet about each and every one of them.

I'm mentioning them here because you can use each of these tools to connect better with the Sacred Flames and the Divine Rays.

All of these subjects can be studied individually, and the techniques and information that you learn will most definitely benefit you in your spiritual development.

I would encourage you to follow your intuition, be discerning, find authors whose energy you align with, find tools and methods that suit you and absorb what you need.

If I had to choose one book to recommend on visualisation, it would be *Creative Visualisation* by Shakti Gawain. This little book changed my life. I came across it in about 1983 and have probably possessed a dozen copies since; I think it is so wonderful I keep giving my copy away to friends!

My go-to crystal experts are Judy Hall and Philip Permutt, who have both published dozens of helpful books. I would also highly recommend Edwin Courtenay's *Crystals to Go*.

I have added some information on plants as allies in Section 4 at the request of the Patrons.

Prayer, Invocation, Ritual and Affirmation

Prayer, invocation, ritual, and affirmation are individually incredible spiritual tools used by humans throughout the ages.

Put very simply, prayer is an invocation or act that seeks to activate a rapport with an object of worship through deliberate communication.

When we pray, repeat an invocation, repeat an affirmation, or perform a ritual of any kind, we are communicating, making a request, or perhaps setting an intention.

Physical changes occur within our brain and our physiology, and on a quantum level, we send a pulse of vibratory energy towards the 'object'. We are back to vibration again!

It then follows that because of the Law of Attraction, what we receive back from this 'pulse of energy' depends on our own vibration. This is my personal understanding, a simplistic view of a hugely complex subject.

We are all unique beings and will all have a unique experience connecting with the Sacred Flames and the Divine Rays. I believe that no experience is less worthy than the another, that we receive or channel what is needed at the time; that this experience will change over time as we change and develop.

So, consider creating your own prayer, invocation or ritual using the words that feel right to you. The Patrons have suggested invocations for the Sacred Flames, but if you are guided to tweak them, do. This is YOUR practice, be guided by your intuition.

Additionally, channelled affirmations for working with each of the Divine Rays can be found in *The Book of Many Colours* and the Divine Ray Oracle & Affirmation Cards.

Past Life Recall

When you connect with the Sacred Flames and Divine Rays, many of you will experience past life recall and remembrance. I would encourage you to journal these recollections and not worry too much about them to start with, as the Patrons have a way of helping you to understand through serendipity and portent.

Reincarnation and past lives are other subjects that hundreds of books have been written about. My first 'teacher' on this subject was Edgar Cayce, and his books are a good place to start if you want a better understanding.

If you do feel a need to make more sense of these experiences, the best guidance you will find is from your own Spirit Guides and Guardian Angel; simply connect with them in prayer or meditation and ask what you need to know.

I've created a downloadable meditation to get you started on my website https://www.cariadspiritual.com/sacredflames

Gratitude & Grounding

It is only polite to say please and thank you! Do remember to ask to connect and thank your guides and guardians and the Patrons for their support and for connecting with you. Their service to us is a divine privilege.

You also need to take care moving from spiritual work back into the everyday world. After every spiritual practice, it is important to ground, centre and reset your energy system to a safe operating level. I tell my students to think of it like hitting the standby button on their TV.

Take some deep breaths, breathe down into the earth, centre yourself, move your body, take a drink of water or eat something, and call in your usual spiritual protection and your Guardian Angel.

Make sure that you are properly grounded before going out into the world and particularly before driving.

Part Two

What It's All About

---

*"If We Fail To Look After Others
When They Need Help,
Who Will Look After Us?"*
Buddha

What Are the Sacred Flames and Divine Rays?

In simple terms, the highest vibrating form of light is pure, clear light and that is the light of the Creator, the 'Divine'. Each Divine Ray represents a different quality of the Divine, their energy present here on Earth. Each of the Divine Rays has an active principle, a Sacred Flame that is the power behind the energy.

As I previously mentioned in *The Book of Many Colours*, at this point, it is important to note that the Rays have changed with time, as our planet has changed and as we have changed. Many great channels have written about the Divine Rays, the Sacred Flames and their functions, and if you feel guided to, research their work further and exercise your own discernment. Intuitively make up your own mind and select your own truth.

So, every schoolchild knows that when you shine a light through a clear crystal, a rainbow of coloured light is refracted through it, and we are all familiar with the colours of the rainbows that light our skies after the rain.

Similarly, the colours of the Divine Rays are the aspects of the Divine, energy that radiates down to our planet for the purpose of supporting All that there is. What follows in these pages is practical guidance on how to tap into this energy, together with personal messages from the Patrons on the use of the Sacred Flames for personal development and healing.

Each Sacred Flame is the active principle of a Divine Ray which has a unique number, name, properties, colour, symbol, Patron, active principle and crystal energy that aligns with it. *(There are also Archangels, Archaea and other light beings that serve on the Rays, but I intend to keep it simple.)*

There is a key difference between working with the energy of the Divine Rays and invoking the Sacred Flames. When you are bathed in the energy of the Divine Rays the feeling is more passive, more feminine, whilst when you invoke the energy of the Sacred Flames, be prepared for a greater vibrational shift, a more direct and masculine energy (which the Patrons assert is ideal for healing).

Having said that, each has significant power, so the choice of how to work with these energies rests with you. Remember to exercise your discernment and to follow your intuition.

Who Are The Patrons of The Divine Rays?

There is a spiritual hierarchy that governs and supports life in our Universe and on this planet, which functions as a complex government. This is a huge subject, but very simply, the light beings that fulfil the roles of Patrons of the Divine Rays are Cosmic Ascended Masters, Ascended Masters, Lady Ascended Masters, Archangels and Archangelic Collectives. The beings who occupy these important roles as Patrons of the Divine Rays and their Esoteric Fires are considered to be among the most highly evolved beings in our Universe.

Don't let fear of being worthy put you off here. If you've picked up this book then you are ready to work with these energies and magnificent beings of light. No matter where you are on your spiritual journey connecting to these amazing energies will bring wisdom and light into your life. Believe me, your life will never be the same again!

I won't be going into long descriptions about each of the Patrons. There is so much information readily available, but what I would say is, be discerning about what you accept as truth.

How To Choose Which Sacred Flame To Invoke

There are several ways you can choose which Sacred Flame or Divine Ray energy to work with.

This list is not exhaustive. It simply represents ideas to help you choose how to work with these energies. You should always be guided intuitively on what feels right for you (or your client if you are already an established energy healer or channel):

- Intuitively, by asking for guidance and simply by opening this book
- By first choosing (or being chosen by) a Patron – you will find a quick list in Part Four - and connect to the Sacred Flame they patronise
- By choosing a colour you are drawn to
- By choosing a symbol that 'jumps out at you'
- By identifying an issue you would like support with
- Intuitively selecting a particular Sacred Flame to channel healing energy to another person, animal, or place

Divine Ray Oracle & Affirmation Cards are also available from www.cariadspiritual.com/shop to accompany this book and can also be used as a tool for selecting which energy to work with for the self or others.

Channelling Healing Energy For Others

I first trained as an energy healer in 1985, so in this life, scarily, I've had almost 40 years' experience of channelling healing energy for the benefit of others. I first worked as a spiritual healer, simply opening myself up as a channel to the Divine and allowing the healing energy to flow where needed. I have since been attuned to, and become a practitioner and Master Teacher of several different healing modalities, including Angelic Reiki, Divine Energy Healing, Violet Flame Rescue Flames Healing, Pendragon Reiki and several others; I have also been blessed as the channel of Ninth Ray Reiki.

Every healing vibration is different. Many healers are attuned to different modalities so that they are able to offer the energy that suits the vibration of the person that they are working with and what they need at the time. Here is a very brief overview of how it all works and some guidance on becoming a clear channel for energy for the benefit of self and others.

What every healing modality has in common is that the healer becomes a channel for energy from the Divine, source, the universe or whatever is your belief.

This healing energy is intelligent and promotes the well-being and restoration of balance holistically in the mind, body, or spirit of the recipient.

The healer connects to an energy source and the healing energy is drawn through the healer's physical and energetic system, through their energy channels, meridians and chakras and usually out through the hands (though sometimes through the heart or solar plexus chakra).

There is a great deal of legislation, many rules and regulations, guidance and best practice that has been put into place to protect both professional healers and their clients.

The guidance on healing contained within these pages is aimed at those who wish to channel healing energy for friends, family and for the benefit of All that there is.

Working with these powerful esoteric energies will also be of considerable benefit to those who are already professionally trained in the healing arts; adding a fantastic tool to your energetic toolbox to assist your clients.

Clearly, if you are considering a professional healing career, you will need formal training, insurance etc, in order to practice.

However, I believe that the best healers are those who very simply want to make a positive difference to the well-being of another; intention is the key.

Allowing yourself to be the channel through which healing energy flows is one of the most precious gifts that you can give another.

It is important not to compare yourself and your experience of channelling healing energy to anybody else; we are all unique beings and will have different experiences. Do not think that because you have not felt anything, or your recipient has not felt anything, that nothing has happened. Healing energy works holistically on mind, body and soul, so if you have approached the practice with a pure intention, it will work positively on some level and cannot cause harm.

In *The Book of Many Colours,* I shared how my channelling abilities switched on, like the flick of a switch. This may be the case for you, or it may not, and you may not feel or see anything. It truly depends on your unique vibration and past life experiences, as your soul remembers who you truly are.

Please never feel that you have not been of service or failed in any way. There are many factors that come into play when healing energy is channelled; the will of the Divine and the will of the Higher Self of the recipient in particular.

'Fixing' another person is not your responsibility, and letting go of any preconceived ideas of the outcome of your healing session is the best way to approach it.

I tell my students to learn to disengage their consciousness and feel as if they are "standing behind themselves" allowing the energy to flow through them as a channel and do its work.

In my experience, working as an energy healer also leaves you feeling pretty amazing because of the residual energy that remains and moves within your own physical and energetic systems after channelling healing.

The Patrons are keen that the Esoteric Fires are used as a healing resource and that as many people as possible are awakened to their potential.

Therefore, if you have had no training in healing whatsoever, here you will find some simple guidance to point you in the right direction to channel the Sacred Flames safely and responsibly.

There is clear guidance in this section on preparation of the self, very simple but important steps, and a straightforward process to follow for your own comfort and protection.

It is very important that the healer should have attended to their own physical and spiritual hygiene before considering channelling healing for somebody else; avoiding strong-smelling perfume if you are working hands-on, and always ensuring you are free from negative energy that might interfere with being a clear channel.

The relaxation and energetic clearing that follows is a really important step before you start. Equally as important is letting go of any thoughts of the outcome of your practice; healing energy is intelligent and goes where it is needed.

It is important to ask permission from the person you wish to send healing energy to; we have free will and it is up to them whether or not they choose to receive it.

If you cannot obtain that permission for some reason or are sending the healing energy to a group, a place, the planet etc, it is my view that adding this clause should ensure you do not incur any karmic repercussions:

I request the highest quality healing energy for (name)

for the highest good of all and harm of none,

in accordance with the will of the Divine and will of the higher self.

You may wish to use this clause to preface all of your healing sessions; in this way, you assert your intention for being the channel for the highest quality healing energy possible.

Distant, Absent and Hands-On Healing

There is absolutely no difference in the quality of the healing energy received by the recipient if you are working in their presence or from the other side of the planet.

Here are the differences between the approaches:

- ❈ Absent healing is sent to the recipient from a separate location. I have worked this way for many years with clients all over the world; feedback from these clients and from those who visit me in person for healing is exactly the same.

✤ Distant healing can be sent to a recipient who is in the same room, but the healer does not physically touch the recipient. Some healers work a few inches above the body in the auric field, whilst others may sit close by and channel energy. This method is particularly useful if the person you are working with is in great physical pain or does not wish to be touched.

✤ Hands-on healing is just that! Rules and regulations have changed considerably in the near 40 years that I have been working as an energy healer. Today, most insurers require healers to work with their hands placed lightly on the shoulders or with the left hand on the higher heart chakra and the right hand on the solar plexus.

These changes have come into place because of abuse and are for the protection of both healer and recipient. Therefore, a healer should **always** ask the permission of the recipient before placing their hands anywhere on the body and check that the weight of the hands is comfortable for the recipient.

Additionally, if you are giving healing to a child under 16, to a vulnerable person etc, it is necessary for a chaperone to be present. There is absolutely no reason why any clothes, other than perhaps an overcoat, need to be removed for healing sessions.

How To Invoke the Sacred Flames

Before you begin, take a moment to understand the enormous privilege that is being bestowed on you. Approach your practice with reverence; it is sacred work!

There is no need to spend hours in prayer beforehand; simply an appreciation of the sanctity of what you are doing is enough.

We all lead such busy lives in the 21st century, and for most of us, our minds are constantly busy. What we aim for in this practice is calming the 'monkey mind', learning to find quiet and space to allow divine connection and to become a clear channel for this sacred energy.

I do not want to preach to the converted, but if you have never meditated or channelled healing energy before, here are some helpful tips:

Find a comfortable space where you will not be disturbed. Turn off any unnecessary electronic gadgets and move them to another room. Get comfy and prepare to sit or lie still for a few minutes. If you are brand new to channelling energy, start with 10 minutes and work your way up. Eventually, aim for half an hour. This is about the right amount of time for most people to connect to high vibrational energy.

Tip

Gather any appropriate crystals and place them nearby. You might like a pillow or blanket to hand, and remember to have a glass of water ready. It's also a good idea to set an alarm.

Bathing in sacred sound is a beautiful way to settle into your connection. I am a huge fan of the Solfeggio frequencies, the frequencies of our universe in sound, and there are so many free tracks available on YouTube. Be intuitive about your selection. Good ones to start with are 432 Hertz and 528 Hertz tracks.

Tip

Use headphones to block out any external noise and distractions. It's also helpful to have an electromagnetic shield if you're using a mobile phone. Shungite is a fantastic crystal for this; be mindful of the supplier of any crystal you purchase. Please ensure it has been ethically sourced.

Being cocooned in sacred oil vibrations during your connection is a glorious addition to this practice. Again, be intuitive in your selection and ensure that any oils you use are of the highest quality affordable.

Tip

I have a range of Alchemical Aura Sprays attuned to the Sacred Flames available on my website (www.cariadspiritual.com), the recipes for which have been channelled and are attuned to the Sacred Flames and their crystal counterparts.

Remember your Spiritual Protection (see page 14). Decide which Sacred Flame you wish to connect to and your intention, whether this is for the benefit of self, others or All that there is.

Tip

*It's **very** important to set a specific intention.*

Follow the process overpage to channel the energy of the Sacred Flame.

The Process

- Relax and energetically clear yourself
- Ground
- Call in your guides and guardians
- Visualise the sacred symbol
- Invoke the Sacred Flame
- Intend the energy and allow it to flow where intended
- Cease the flow and disconnect your energy
- Give thanks to the Patrons, guides and guardians
- Feedback and record-keeping

Relax And Energetically Clear Yourself

We will use the breath to relax deeply and move relaxation through the physical body by way of the energy centres (chakras) preparing you for this connection.

Cleansing, clearing, relaxing, releasing, healing and harmonising, connecting you to All that there is, relaxing the physical, and shifting any negative or stuck energy in the subtle energy body.

Take at least two breaths at each chakra, be intuitive if you need to release more tension or stuck energy, then do so and feel the energy flow downwards.

It is useful to visualise the chakras as Catherine Wheels, seeing sparks of stuck energy drifting away to be grounded into Mother Earth, to be repurposed, recycled, and reused.

Make your body comfortable, roll back your shoulders and gently move your neck to release any tension. Make sure that your arms and legs are uncrossed, and if sitting, connect your feet with the floor beneath you.

Breathe deeply. In through your nose and out through your mouth, deep into your lungs. For a moment, simply be aware of the rise and fall of your belly.

Now, deepen the relaxation.

Breathe in for the count of three, hold for three, breathe out for three. (Repeat three times.)

Breathe in for the count of four, hold for four, breathe out for four. (Repeat three times.)

Start to feel waves of relaxation moving down over your physical body, starting at your Crown, the top of your head. Expand this chakra with your breath, cleansing, clearing, relaxing, releasing, healing, and harmonising. See the chakra spinning, clearing any stuck energy, and watch it rain down upon the Earth. Take as many breaths as you need before you move your breath with intention, down your body to the next chakra. Feel these waves begin to relax every hair on your head.

Move these waves of relaxation with your breath, down to your Brow Chakra in the centre of your forehead, your Third Eye. Expand this chakra with your breath, cleansing, clearing, relaxing, releasing, healing, and harmonising. See the chakra spinning, clearing any stuck energy, and watch it rain down upon the Earth. Take as many breaths as you need before you move your breath with intention down your body.

Move your attention to your Throat Chakra in the centre of your throat. Expand this chakra with your breath, cleansing, clearing, relaxing, releasing, healing, and harmonising. See the chakra spinning, clearing any stuck energy, and watch it rain down upon the Earth. Take as many breaths as you need before you move your breath with intention down your body.

Attend now to the shoulders, arms, hands, and fingers. Release any tension, allowing your breath to travel down, releasing tension, feeling it drifting away, returning it to Mother Earth.

Move your attention to your Heart Chakra in the centre of your chest. Expand this chakra with your breath, cleansing, clearing, relaxing, releasing, healing, and harmonising. See the chakra spinning, clearing any stuck energy, and watch it rain down upon the Earth. Take as many breaths as you need before you move your breath with intention down your body.

Move down to your Solar Plexus Chakra a few inches above your tummy button. Expand this chakra with your breath, cleansing, clearing, relaxing, releasing, healing, and harmonising. See the chakra spinning, clearing any stuck energy, and watch it rain down upon the Earth. Take as many breaths as you need before you move your breath with intention down your body.

Move down to your Sacral Chakra in the core of your belly. Expand the chakra with your breath, cleansing, clearing, relaxing, releasing, healing, and harmonising. See the chakra spinning, clearing any stuck energy, and watch it rain down upon the Earth. Take as many breaths as you need before you move your breath with intention down your body.

Move next to your Root Chakra at the base of your spine. Expand the chakra with your breath, cleansing, clearing, relaxing, releasing, healing, and harmonising. See the chakra spinning, clearing any stuck energy and watching it rain down upon the Earth. Take as many breaths as you need before you move your breath with intention down your body.

Now, draw this relaxing energy down your thighs, past your knees, shins, calves, ankles, feet, and toes, grounding all remaining negative or stuck energy into Mother Earth to be repurposed, recycled, reborn.

Ground

Take a moment now to ground yourself by imagining roots emanating from the soles of your feet and moving deeply into Mother Earth, weaving through the layers of earth, water, rock, and crystal until they reach the centre of the Earth and the crystal of the Divine Ray and Sacred Flame you have chosen to connect with.

Call In Your Guides And Guardians

Simply ask your Guardian Angel and the guides who support you to join you (if you have another Angel or deity you'd like to join, you can ask them too).

Visualise The Sacred Symbol

Now, bring into your mind's eye the shape or symbol associated with the Sacred Flame. If it is a shape, visualise that shape around you and transform it into three dimensions so that you are sitting within it. If it is a symbol, visualise that symbol in front of you and draw it in towards you, allowing it to rest where it feels comfortable.

Invoke The Sacred Flame

Next, send your intention upwards to the Creator and invoke the Sacred Flame of your choice.

Invocations for each Sacred Flame are found in Part 3. Visualise the energy flowing as follows:

Visualise the colour of the Sacred Flame and feel the energy flowing down through your transpersonal chakras, the Stellar Gateway, and Soul Star Chakras above your head, into your Crown Chakra, and moving downwards through your body to the Solar

Plexus, then flowing back up, through the arms and out the through the palms of your hands.

Intend The Energy And Allow It To Flow Where Intended

Be specific in your request. If you do not have permission, ensure you use the following safety clause:

I request healing energy for (name)

for the highest good of all and harm of none,

in accordance with the will of the Divine and the higher self.

Visualise the person, place, being bathed in the energy of the Sacred Flame. Let go of any thoughts of the outcome. Simply allow the energy to flow where it is needed.

You may feel tingling in your hands or a change in temperature around you; this is perfectly normal.

Cease the Flow and Disconnect your Energy

The energy should simply cease to flow automatically.

When it does, it is very important to **consciously assert** that you are disconnected from the person, group, place you were sending the healing energy to.

Give Thanks to the Patrons, Guides and Guardians

With deepest gratitude for this communion, give thanks to the Patron who has graced you with their presence and the sacred energy that has been channelled; thank your Guardian Angel, guides and any beings of light that have supported you with this healing.

Ground yourself by taking some deep breaths into your solar plexus and sacral chakra, call in your usual spiritual protection and take a sip of water.

Note: You are responsible for managing your own energy, and it is important that you are fully present and grounded before going out into the world.

Feedback and Record-Keeping

Obviously, if you are a professional healer, you will be familiar with the requirements to keep notes of your healing sessions and have a practice of chatting to your client afterwards, discussing their feedback and ensuring that they are fully hydrated and grounded after receiving energy healing.

If you are new to channelling healing energy, you may wish to do the same.

Anchoring The Light Of The Sacred Flames

The marvellous Edwin Courtenay suggested this method of anchoring the light of the Sacred Flames by empowering candle flames with the Esoteric Fires.

Calling them into the flames of the candle so that as they burn, they anchor and hold the light and energy of the Sacred Fires into our homes and space. This is a little like using crystals as anchor points but more transitory. You could light a different candle every day and call upon a different Flame.

You could even pass this blessing (or sacred energy connection) on from candle to candle by lighting another virgin candle from your dedicated flame; perpetuating the blessing and even passing on a dedicated candle as a beautiful gift of light to another person. Please remember safety when using candles in your home or therapy space.

I have created a community on Facebook so you can share experiences with others who are working with the Sacred Flames and Divine Ray energy. It can be found here:

https://www.facebook.com/groups/193813969564198

In Part Three, you will find detailed information about the Sacred Flames, channelled messages from each of the Patrons and lots more information and inspiration.

Part Three

The Sacred Flames & The Divine Rays

*"Set your life on fire
Seek those who fan your flames."*

Rumi

"…be guided by higher powers…set aside ego and simply become a channel in service for love of all."

The Cosmic Ascended Master Sanat Kumara
Channelled by Angela Orora Medway-Smith
The Book of Many Colours, **August 2020**

The Flame of Divine Service
(incorporating Divine Surrender and Divine Love)
The 1ˢᵗ Ray
The Ray of the Avatar

Patron:	The Master Jesus
Colour:	Ruby Red
Shape:	The Single Pillar

Properties: Manifestation, energetic grounding, anchoring and embodiment. The Ray of the 'Master Builder'. Those who incarnate under this ray do so in order to create something meaningful and powerful for the world. Alignment and communion with the Divine Father, self-mastery through dedication, service, ritual, and practice. The masculine Christ energy the Christos – Passion. The Animus – masculine self.

Invocation:

Creator, I AM spirit bright

Round me burn your flame of light

From Ascended Master Flame, called forth now in your name

I invoke the Flame of Divine Service

Guarded and guided by the Master Jesus

To (insert your intention here)

With pure intent for the highest outcome and harm of none

In accordance with your will and the Divine plan

The Master Jesus / Sananda speaks:

Beloved, this Sacred Flame has many distinct layers, these layers incorporate different elements of Divine Love and will bring forward in the seeker what is required for self, others and All that there is.

SELF

I am the Master Jesus. The seeker might ask me to step forth to support them in their endeavour to be of service, to be of support to others.

It is not necessary to remove oneself from society in order to fully embody the energy of service or to live a life of dedication to prayer. Indeed one can be of more service to one's community and to humanity as a whole by recognising that service given in practical fashion is much more valuable.

I give the example of the Ascended Master once known as Mother Teresa; this dear soul has joined the ranks of the Ascended Masters at Shambala. Her earthly life was one spent in service; one might assume that what brought her to such service was her dedication to prayer. Indeed not! Her pathway was that of service to humanity, her human choices brought her to that path by prayer.

So for the self, the energy that steps forward with the Flame of Divine Love is that which can support you to align to your true destiny; your soul's purpose in respect of service to the Divine.

Invoke this ray and flame when you wish to receive clarity, when you wish to receive direction for oneself.

OTHERS

You may wish to invoke the energy of the Flame of Divine Love to assist those who are in need of surrendering to their destiny, to assist those in need of guidance on their true purpose, their true path in this life.

These may be individuals or small groups of people who you feel are hedging in a direction that does not align with the will of the Divine.

As in all things, when directing this Flame, ensure that you request healing, guidance, inspiration, is intended for the highest good of all and harm of none in accordance with the will of the Divine and the higher self, the soul. Ensuring, this way that you are not imposing your will on others, for this dear soul so may bring karmic repercussions.

ALL THAT THERE IS

The love of the Divine is freely available. You may direct it to All that there is.

This energy, this Sacred Flame has a masculine force that can enable manifestation, it can enable alignment with the will of the Divine, the power of this Sacred Flame is unlimited, as is the case with all the Sacred Flames.

Be mindful beloved one of why you choose to utilise this energy.

Be not impetuous. Sit and meditate on the probable outcome for others and All that there is when you engage with the Flame of Divine Love, Divine Service and Surrender.

The Flame of Grace
The 2nd Ray
The Ray of Grace

Patron: The Master Serapis Bey
Colour: Selenite White
Shape: The Two Pillars

Properties: Flow, the path of least resistance, acceptance, and intuition. Go with the flow! The angelic frequency, communion with Angels, Angelic mediumship, the wisdom of the Angels. Synchronicity, serendipity, Divine guidance, and opportunity. The Divine Gift.

Invocation:

Creator, I AM spirit bright

Round me burn your flame of light

From Ascended Master Flame

Called forth now in your name

I invoke the Flame of Grace

Guarded and guided by the Master Serapis Bey

To (insert your intention here)

With pure intent for the highest outcome and harm of none

In accordance with your will and the Divine plan

The Master Serapis Bey speaks:

Dearest one, this is an auspicious day. One that you will look back on and acknowledge hereafter!

I am Serapis Bay and I bring you Flame of Grace. I am Patron of the Ray of Grace, my tasks are many.

SELF

Should you wish, dear soul, to live your life in a state of grace, call up on this Sacred Ray. Riding on its energy will enable you to navigate the waves of your human life, sailing effortlessly towards your soul's purpose.

Be aware there is a need for you to connect on a deep level with your higher self, your soul, to understand your purpose here. In doing so, and in listening to the guidance of your soul, the guidance by which you can complete your tasks in this incarnation. Listen, truly listen, and act on that guidance.

Should you wish to commune with my brethren in the Angelic Realm, sit within the energy of this Ray, call this Flame in sessions during which you master your connection.

For to be a true channel, you must learn to put aside your human frailties and rejoice in being of service to those who hold the well-being of mankind in their hearts.

OTHERS

You may invoke the Flame of Grace and intend to direct this gentle yet powerful energy to those who seek or require healing; those whose lives are chaotic. The vibrations of this Sacred Flame will enable them to rise above the dross of their human experience.

ALL THAT THERE IS

It would be wise, beloved, to work together with others with the Flame of Grace if the intention is to send to All that there is.

It can be manifested for the greater good of all and alignment with other Sacred Flames. For example, should you wish to direct the energy of the Ray of Challenge forward to support those groups of beings to deal with transition (or your planet herself indeed) you may request the support of the Flame of Grace to accompany this energy. See how they weave together in order to seamlessly gracefully and naturally bring the change required.

"Beloveds, you have at your fingertips information that can support both your spiritual development and ascension, gifts that can support the wellbeing and healing of All that there is…"

The Ascended Master El Morya
Channelled by Angela Orora Medway-Smith
The Book of Many Colours, **April 2021**

The Magdalene Flame
The 3rd Ray
The Ray of New Beginnings

Patron: The Lady Master Nada (Mary Magdalene)
Colour: Rose Pink
Shape: Triangle

Properties*: Growth, birth, purity, innocence, and awe. The Inner Child. The wisdom of the Divine Feminine – the Sophia – the Feminine Christ force. The power of sacred sound – the song of creation, love, beauty, empathy, and appreciation.

*see also Page 151

Invocation:

Creator, I AM spirit bright
Round me burn your flame of light
From Ascended Master Flame
Called forth now in your name
I invoke the Magdalene Flame
Guarded and guided by Lady Nada
To (insert your intention here)
With pure intent for the highest outcome and harm of none
In accordance with your will and the Divine plan

The Ascended Master Lady Nada speaks:

The energy of the Magdalene Flame is multi-layered; it comprises several distinct vibrations which are all aligned to the wisdom of the Divine Feminine, the Sophia. I, Lady Nada, am Guardian of this Sacred Flame forged during my life as The Magdalene.

SELF

Beloveds, there are many reasons why you might wish to work with the energy of the Magdalene Flame.

It can support you in recovering those long-buried incidents within your childhood that have impacted you and your spiritual development. The Magdalene Flame carries the energy of the Black Madonna, of the Divine Mother of the Feminine Christ Force.

Be guided by your heart, be guided by your intuition; hold not any desirous outcome, intend instead that the Magdalene Flame burns that which does not serve you on all levels of your being.

OTHERS

The invocation of the Magdalene Flame for others can achieve everything described for self!

Simply follow your intuition, beloved! Intend the Magdalene Flame for those you feel require access to the wisdom of the divine feminine and appreciation of their role on this earthly path.

ALL THAT THERE IS

Oh beloved!

The wisdom carried by the Magdalene Flame is beneficial to all of humankind. It can assist in the restoration of innocence and awe and encourage those recipients to lighten their load.

The power of the individual elements contained within the Magdalene Flame burns through the unnecessary human constructs that prevent growth and, as such, creates new beginnings.

> *"Are you ready?*
> *This is your time — the time of enlightenment.*
> *You can choose whether to sit, remain in your current position and be blind to the possibilities or to embrace them.*
> *As always, it is your choice…"*

The Ascended Master St Germain
Channelled by Angela Orora Medway-Smith
The Book of Many Colours, August 2020

The Flame of Mastery
The 4th Ray
The Ray of the Spiritual Warrior

Patron: The Master El Morya (King Arthur)

Colour: Royal Blue

Shape: Square

Properties: Stability, physical grounding, strength, strategy, leadership, discipline. Masculine – solar – dynamic force. The way of self-mastery - the way of the spiritual warrior – champion of the light, defender of the weak, the clearing of negative energies and entities. The Will of the Divine.

Invocation:

Creator, I AM spirit bright

Round me burn your flame of light

From Ascended Master Flame

Called forth now in your name

I invoke the Flame of Mastery

Guarded and guided by the Master El Morya

To (insert your intention here)

With pure intent for the highest outcome and harm of none

In accordance with your will and the Divine plan

The Ascended Master El-Morya speaks:

I am the Ascended Master El Morya, and I step forward to support mankind with the Flame of Mastery and the Ray of Mastery.

SELF

Children, I will stand by your side when you stand for right and justice. Call on me, invoke the Flame of Mastery for support with many things.

As its name might suggest, to be supported in mastering a skill. This Sacred Flame is of great benefit for those who wish to lead and to teach; its energy can support you to excel in these actions.

Understand assistance will be given to those who are worthy, ensuring that your request is made with integrity and the intention of highest good of all is essential.

When you stand for right and justice and require an ally, invoke my presence and it shall be so.

OTHERS

Beloveds, when you join with others marching for freedom, marching for justice, marching for right and a just cause supporting the greater good, call on the Flame of Mastery.

Call on me, my brothers and sisters, and I will support you to stand, to fight for your cause.

Additionally, you may invoke the Flame of Mastery, you may invoke my presence, to support your leaders to support your teachers who work for the highest good of all.

ALL THAT THERE IS

On a global scale, the Flame of Mastery can be invoked to support all leaders, to follow the path of righteousness, to follow actions that are for the highest good of all.

One aspect that requires this support at the moment is dealing with the change of the climate on Earth. You can choose to invoke the Flame of Mastery to support its leaders.

The ramifications of the actions of mankind are great, the cessation of the activities that cause climate change can be requested. Simply invoke the Flame of Mastery, intend that its energy will support mankind's leaders to do the right thing and I will add my energy to this cause.

It seems that children are awakened to this issue; it is time that ALL mankind understands their part! I and Flame of Mastery can be of assistance.

Do not believe that you have no power in this case, indeed your power is great when you invoke this energy.

Inspiration and guidance will be given to those who seek and those who follow those for whom the energy of this Flame is intended.

*"...I implore you to love one another
This simple action brings healing to all..."*

The Master Jesus

Channelled by Angela Orora Medway-Smith

The Book of Many Colours, **April 2021**

The Flame of Unification
The 5th Ray
The Ray of Unity

Properties: The Master Kuthumi (St Francis of Assisi)

Colour: Butter Yellow

Shape: The Pentacle/Pentagon

Properties: Equilibrium and balance, the classical elements, the holistic perspective. Unity consciousness and interconnection, the tapestry of life. Relationships and mediation, the life streams of the world, self-awareness, self-knowledge, internal dialogue. The acknowledgement that the Divine is to be found in all living things.

Invocation:

Creator, I AM spirit bright

Round me burn your flame of light

From Ascended Master Flame

Called forth now in your name

I invoke the Flame of Unification

Guarded and guided by the Master Kuthumi

To (insert your intention here)

With pure intent for the highest outcome and harm of none

In accordance with your will and the Divine plan

The Master Kuthumi speaks:

I, Kuthumi, bring you the Flame of Unification.

SELF

Divine Soul, seeker, for the self bathe within the energy of this ray, focus on the Flame of Unification when you wish to remember your place in this Divine Plan. Guidance will be forthcoming on how you might impact the betterment of all. Your role in that; do not underestimate your role in the Divine Plan, request my support, request my guidance, done with an open heart it will be so!

OTHERS

Should you feel guided, you may request this connection for others by invoking the Flame of Unification. To assist them in seeing, being shown their part in the Divine Plan, giving them confidence in the ability to support the highest good of all.

Be guided, dearest soul, as to whom you should send this support.

ALL THAT THERE IS

Beloved! Such is the fragmentation in the ranks of humanity, this Sacred Flame is much needed by mankind at this time.

Not simply for unification amongst brethren but also to recognise the impact each individual soul has on both the consciousness and health of All that there is.

I speak of your planet; I speak of the avoidable tragedy that looms*.

Gather together brothers and sisters. Be the change, unify the consciousness of humanity in this!

*climate change

*"....You are love,
crafted with love by the Creator,
be that love,
BE ONLY LOVE."*

The Archangelic Collective The Cherubim
Channelled by Angela Orora Medway-Smith
The Book of Many Colours, April 2021

The Flame of Nurture
The 6th Ray
The Ray of the Divine Mother

Patron: The Lady Master – Mother Mary

Colour: Madonna Blue

Shape: Hexagram/Hexagon (Six-Pointed Star)

Properties: Nurturing, healing, unconditional love, evocation, and comfort. The Goddess mysteries, the Divine Mother (Shekinah) and the Tree of Knowledge. Service, duty, purpose, and restraint; self-possession. Introspection, meditation, silence, and retreat – the power of going within. Restoration, rest, and peace.

Invocation:

Creator, I AM spirit bright

Round me burn your flame of light

From Ascended Master Flame

Called forth now in your name

I invoke the Flame of Nurture

Guarded and guided by the Mother Mary

To (insert your intention here)

With pure intent for the highest outcome and harm of none

In accordance with your will and the Divine plan

The Lady Master Mary speaks:

Sisters and brothers welcome! My love for you, the love of the Divine for you, is infinite.

We Ascended Master and Angelic Collectors step forward in service to mankind with everything that the Divine makes available to you in order that you live your human life in the best possible way.

For the past 2000 years, humanity has revered me, my wish is that you see me not only as Mother but as Priestess and ally.

SELF

Beloved, you may invoke the Flame of Nurture for comfort, support, healing, to feel my unconditional love and the unconditional love of the Divine surround you and support you.

You may also invoke my presence to assist with the purpose of going within; this can be for guidance examination of actions or simply to rest and recuperate in love.

I support those who serve, providing guidance and enlightenment and assisting those beings of light who wish to be of service to the Divine to align with their souls' past path, their mission in this life.

OTHERS

You may intend to invoke the Flame of Nurture for others in all that is described above. Be ever mindful of the need for nurture, the need for rest, the need for clarity on the path of service. All this can be achieved within the Ray of Nurture. When you invoke this Sacred Flame, I lend my energy and support to your mission.

ALL THAT THERE IS

You may, dear soul, intend this energy to be spread across all humanity, all sentient beings, indeed all dimensions of your reality; be they within the plant kingdom, animal kingdom or elsewhere. Sent with the highest intention, you may invoke the Cherubim to join their energy to the Flame of Nurture with the Flame of Divine Love, also invoking the Flame of Interconnectedness!

So much can be achieved, beloved! Understand your power when you work with the Sacred Flames for the highest good of all. This is limitless!

*"Beloveds, brothers and sisters of light,
understand that the Silver Violet Flame has a separate
and distinct energy
to the Violet Flame itself.
It carries deep codes of magic, and these threads of ancient
magic reborn in Avalon rise again, held in the hearts of
beacons of light on the planet at this time...."*

**The Ascended Master Lady Portia
Channelled by Angela Orora Medway-Smith**
The Book of Many Colours, **April 2021**

The Violet Flame
The 7th Ray
The Ray of Spiritual Alchemy

Patron: The Ascended Master St Germain

Colour: Violet (Amethyst Purple)

Shape: The Heptagon/Heptagram (Seven-Pointed Star)

Properties: Change, transformation, alchemy, clearing and transmutation (the process and journey of change) and its catalytic quickening. Magick, ceremony, ritual, and initiation, perception, vision, clairvoyance and mysticism. Those who 'trigger' others into self-exploration and the possibility of personal change.

Invocation:

Creator, I AM spirit bright

Round me burn your flame of light

From Ascended Master Flame

Called forth now in your name

I invoke the Violet Flame

Guarded and guided by St Germain

To (insert your intention here)

With pure intent for the highest outcome and harm of none

In accordance with your will and the Divine plan

The Ascended Master St Germain speaks:

Dearest ones, we meet again!

Many of you already understand the unique power of the Violet Flame. For millennia, man has been instructed in its use. For almost two hundred years, I have sought to bring this transformational energy into the consciousness of mankind.

Here I will elaborate on how it can be used for self, for others and for the benefit of All that there is.

SELF

Be advised that this, like all of the Sacred Flames, with intention, can be sent backward in time to support your ancestors, sent forwards in time to support your children and your children's children or used in the present for self-healing, for cleansing of toxins, for transmuting negativity and for transforming situations in the current time.

Some also use the Violet Flame to clear a path in traffic, which I find most amusing! But, dearest one, it works! If you invoke the Violet Flame your travels will be smooth, obstacles will be removed from your path. You may encounter delays, but those delays are for your safety and to enable smooth passage.

Obviously, when healing the self, this energy can be summoned to cleanse and clear all of those negative energies that might bring you disharmony on your daily path or, indeed, your soul's path. Understand the power of the Violet Flame as a daily support.

OTHERS

I need to draw your attention to an Awakening that can support you further. The Violet Flame Chakra is a portal in your energetic body that is available to you to reach the elements of the Violet Flame that have previously been unreachable by most.

Many are Awakened and can afford you this privilege. This medium was also instructed to ensure that the healing elements of this Violet Flame would be continued to be received favourably by mankind and therefore accredited this system as a healing modality.

Should you wish to use the Violet Flame for the benefit of others, there are several options available to you. Invoke the Violet Flame itself. It will bring transformation and transmutation of negative energies to the person that you send it to if sent with the right intention.

If you wish, however, to access deeper healing then you would be wise to seek an Awakening of the Violet Flame Chakra in order to channel the Rescue Flames which offer even more power.

ALL THAT THERE IS

The Violet Flame, as with all the Sacred Flames, can be used for the benefit of All that there is. Your intention, beloved, is the key. Intend this energy to support your dear planet, to support its first-

dimensional residents, the stone people; to support its second-dimensional residents, the plant kingdom and of course those animals, insects, birds and human residents of this planet in your third-dimensional reality.

Be assured when requesting the power of this Flame, invoking it for the highest good of all and harm of none, karmically can be of immense benefit.

When you feel that a group of persons, a building, a place, a country or even the entire planet herself, needs the energy of transmutation and transformation, invoke this Flame, request my assistance, and it will be so.

The Flame of Compassion
The 8th Ray
The Ray of Harmony

Patron: The Masters Kwan Yin & Djwhal Khul

Colour: Jade Green

Shape: Octagon/Octagram (Eight-Pointed Star)

Properties: Chaos leading to order, order leading to chaos – the swing of the pendulum, the power of opposites, the cycle of duality and polarity – the lessons of impermanence. The potential for peace, tranquillity, balance and calm, the constancy of movement, and eternity. Exorcism, banishment and compassion.

Invocation:

Creator, I AM spirit bright

Round me burn your flame of light

From Ascended Master Flame

Called forth now in your name

I invoke the Flame of Compassion

Guarded and guided by the Masters Kwan Yin and Djwhal Khul

To (insert your intention here)

With pure intent for the highest outcome and harm of none

In accordance with your will and the Divine plan

The Lady Master Kwan Yin speaks:

Beloveds, brothers and sisters, I am the Ascended Master Kwan Yin. I and my brother Djwhal Khul come to you this day to elaborate on the utilisation of the Flame of Compassion. This Flame can assist with much; it has the power to 'swing the pendulum' from chaos to order. Use its energy wisely.

SELF

Dearest soul do not judge others for their actions. Treat them with compassion, for your understanding of their perspective may not be their view. For it is seen that when several view an event, all have different perceptions, all feel and think differently because of their unique experiences both in this life, in the DNA which recalls the past trauma of their ancestors and their own past life experience.

Use the Flame of Compassion on the self to assist you in non-judgement. Use the Flame of Compassion for the self to assist you in establishing peace and tranquility in your life. Use the Flame of Compassion to enable the swing of the pendulum to move your life, your human path, to a place of tranquility.

OTHERS

That which is described above can also be intended for those you seek to support. Additionally, if you choose to repatriate souls or entities, this Flame can assist with their banishment; that it be done so in **compassion***.*

ALL THAT THERE IS

Divine Soul, you may choose to invoke the Flame of Compassion for all of humanity for all sentient beings; utilise the Flame of Interconnectedness to spread this energy not simply on this planet but throughout your universe as a whole.

Remember that the Sacred Flames can be sent backward in time to assist ancestors or forward in time to assist your descendants; the Elohim may assist with this task.

There is no situation that cannot benefit from the energy of compassion. You may intend that the Flame of Compassion be sent to a situation as well as All that there is.

The Master Djwhal Khul speaks:

I am Djwhal Khul. My sister has spoken. Heed her words.

If your energy aligns with that of mine and you are guided to call upon my presence to support you with the Flame of Compassion then clearly you must do so.

You may also invoke both our presences to assist you in your endeavours. We bring much love and many blessings to you all divine souls.

The Silver Violet Flame
The 9th Ray
The Ray of Challenge

Patron: The Lady Master Portia

Colour: Magenta

Shape: Nonagon/Nonagram (Nine-Pointed Star)

Properties: Challenge, initiation, and opportunity. The deep feminine mysteries, magic, mediumship and seership. Transition and passage from one state/place to another, altered states, consciousness/trance. The shadow and its refinement and acceptance (NOT transformation), introspection, psychism, intuition and sensuality (they are connected).

Invocation:

Creator, I AM spirit bright

Round me burn your flame of light

From Ascended Master Flame

Called forth now in your name

I invoke the Silver Violet Flame

Guarded and guided by the Lady Master Portia

To (insert your intention here)

With pure intent for the highest outcome and harm of none

In accordance with your will and the Divine plan

The Ascended Master Lady Portia speaks:

I am Portia, guardian and Patron of the Silver Violet Flame. My dearest sister, who channels these words, brings you my blessings.

SELF

Beloved, invoke the energy of the Silver Violet Flame for yourself when you are in need of support with challenge. Its energy will bring a softer transformation and transmutation of the energy surrounding your challenge.

Invoke the Silver Violet Flame when you are considering working with your shadow self, to delve deeply into that within your psyche that you have chosen to suppress, be that a dark shadow that you are now seeking to transmute and transform, or the golden element of your shadow that you hide for fear of shining too bright.

The energy of this Flame can also seek to awaken or reawaken those sensual elements of yourself for your betterment. Invoking the Silver Violet Flame can assist in allowing the energies of the kundalini awakening to flow more freely. Your society does not value sensuality as a creative aspect, but my dears, it is so!

Invoke the energy of the Silver Violet Flame and experience how you can bring this aspect of your Self, this aspect of your divinity to support you in creative tasks.

Deep feminine mysteries await when you explore this Flame in calling down and invoking it to support you with your personal development.

OTHERS

For others you may also set the intention to work within the energy of the Silver Violet Flame as described above. Ancient magical codes are embedded within the Silver Violet Flame to enable this.

I step forward with the energies of the New Avalon to guide you bearing the name of Our Lady of Silver. The Silver Violet Flame energy is one of the primary energies that is needed at this time by mankind to support both humanity and your planet.

As with the Violet Flame, an Attunement exists to assist you with the healing of others in the channelling of this Flame and its energies. If you are drawn to healing others using the energy of the Silver Violet Flame you would do well, beloved, to seek more information.

ALL THAT THERE IS

As discussed, the energy of the Silver Violet Flame is a more feminine aspect of the Violet Flame itself. It holds a separate, distinct energy and can gently bring change and transformation to those groups of individuals, places, countries and to the planet herself.

If you are drawn to invoke the Silver Violet Flame for the highest good of all, beloved, call me, invoke my presence, and I will support you with love.

The Flame of Divine Order
The 10th Ray
The Ray of the Divine Father

Patron: Cosmic Ascended Master Maitreya/the Christ

Colour: Pure White

Symbol: The Sun

Properties: God. The Great Central Sun. The Divine Father, the unified Christ energy (male and female combined as one). Genesis, beginning, the creator energies and codes, union with the source, communion, and emergence. The manifest universe; the created reality of time and space.

Invocation:

Creator, I AM spirit bright
Round me burn your flame of light
From Cosmic Ascended Master Flame
Called forth now in your name
I invoke the Flame of Divine Order
Guarded and guided by the Maitreya
To (insert your intention here)
With pure intent for the highest outcome and harm of none
In accordance with your will and the Divine plan

The Cosmic Ascended Master Maitreya / The Christ speaks:

Beloveds, brothers and sisters of light, I will support your endeavours to bring order, to manifest what is required in alignment with the plan of the Divine.

SELF

When you place yourself in the energy of this Divine Ray, when you invoke this Sacred Flame, you are at a soul level requesting that your life be aligned to the Divine plan.

Be therefore ready for a shift; in consciousness, in your life in general, and in how the world perceives you. Working with the energy of this Sacred Flame is not for the faint-hearted.

However, should you invoke this energy for Self, with the acknowledgement that your services for the highest good of all, then it will be so; great riches await.

OTHERS

It would be wise, to avoid any karmic issues, to only invoke this ray, this Sacred Flame, for others with their express permission. The power behind this Sacred Flame is limitless, the power of the Divine is limitless, and you must acknowledge this fact.

ALL THAT THERE IS

Great wisdom, guidance from the Divine, the perfect alignment of the Divine will in All that there is, are the great gifts of invoking this energy.

A practical manifestation of this energy might be prayer, invocation, and the request of guidance for the leaders of your community, the leaders of your world to follow the Divine plan.

Meditation and prayer in groups can accentuate this manifestation, but, dear soul, do not underestimate your own power in these matters when your intention is pure, your request is heard.

Requests of such nature may be supported by invoking the Flame of Universal Consciousness alongside this Sacred Flame. Using this web of interconnectedness to spread the manifestation of your request.

Arise, dearest soul, from your slumber and understand your true purpose!

*"....Children of Light, all that is and has been,
is recorded for your benefit,
for the benefit of all.*

It is accessible to all,
request an audience with one of the guides by tuning into
this Ray, asking me to draw by your side,
and seeing me cut through all irrelevant information..."*

The Archangel Azrael

Channelled by Angela Orora Medway-Smith

***The Book of Many Colours*, April 2021**

* *refers to the Halls of the Akasha*

The Green Flame
The 11th Ray
The Green Ray

Patron: The Archangel Uriel
Colour: Green
Symbol: The Trilithon
(An Archway of Three Stones – A Henge)

Properties: The power of the life cycle, birth, life, death, and decay. The harmony of nature, regeneration, restoration, and renaissance. The earth element and earth elementals (fae, gnomes, dryads, woodwose, the parliament of trees etc), the healing (and magical) power of herbs, flowers, weeds, plants, and trees. Earth wisdom and magic, abundance, physical health and well-being.

Invocation:

Creator, I AM spirit bright

Round me burn your flame of light

From Archangelic Flame

Called forth now in your name

I invoke the Green Flame

Guarded and guided by the Archangel Uriel

To (insert your intention here)

With pure intent for the highest outcome and harm of none

In accordance with your will and the Divine plan

The Archangel Uriel speaks:

Beloveds, as buds unfurl, marvel and be aware of the Green Ray and its power; for without it, life on your planet would cease.

I am Uriel, Angel of Creation, Patron of the Green Ray, Guardian of the Green Flame

SELF

Beloved, you may call upon the energy of the Green Flame for healing of all kinds for self and others. Intend, for example, that it shines more brightly in spaces and places where its invocation will create growth for an individual.

The energy of the Green Flame may be not simply used for healing. It is also a crucible, a 'catalytic converter'; that can enable the seeker to tap into ancient earth wisdom for regeneration of all levels of the self.

OTHERS

The Green Flame may be invoked to support those barren areas; whether that be beings in human form or, areas of land to promote growth in all areas. Additionally, you may intend the Green Ray to permeate, and add its energy to those herbs, sacred oils and healing potions you create for others.

ALL THAT THERE IS

All of the intentions I have spoken of can be undertaken under the Green Flame for the benefit of All that there is.

This, beloved, is ancient energy, present from the dawn of creation.

It is simple to intend the channelling of healing energy from the Green Ray; satisfactory attunements exist in a specific healing modality that would be beneficial to you, so you should be called to follow the path of healer under this Flame.

Many riches can be bestowed on recipients of energy from the Green Flame. Do not underestimate its capacity, beloved.

*"....Children of light,
call upon me for protection,
work with me,
support those who need protecting,
invoke my energy,
let us remove negativity from your world together...."*

**The Archangel Michael
Channelled by Angela Orora Medway-Smith**
The Book of Many Colours, **April 2021**

The Flame of Miracle
The 20th Ray
The Ray of Miracle

Patron: Cosmic Ascended Master Maha Cohan
Colour: Turquoise Blue
Symbol: The Dove

Properties: Connection, communion, communication, and alignment. Synchronicity, serendipity and attunement, the power of miracle. Divine will, service and the spiritual path, inspiration and the inspirer, spiritual teaching, and spiritual healing. Service and sacrifice and the courage required to do both. The Holy Spirit.

Invocation:

Creator, I AM spirit bright

Round me burn your flame of light

From Cosmic Ascended Master Flame

Called forth now in your name

I invoke the Flame of Miracle

Guarded and guided by the Maha Cohan

To (insert your intention here)

With pure intent for the highest outcome and harm of none

In accordance with your will and the Divine plan

The Cosmic Ascended Master Maha Cohan speaks:

The Dove is the symbol of peace the symbol of the Holy Spirit.

I am the Maha Cohan. I bring the Flame of Miracle which can assist you in creating miracles! This Sacred Flame fans the waves of communion, of connection, and brings the seeker inspiration and alignment on the spiritual path whether that is one of healer or teacher.

SELF

One might invoke this Sacred Flame for support in service to the Divine, for the creation of everyday miracles that can support you on your spiritual path. Be creative, dear soul, in your invocation of this energy, obviously ensuring that your intention is for the highest good of all and harm of none; be mindful of karmic consequences of your requests.

OTHERS

Beloved soul, you may support others with the Flame of Miracle in order that they also align with the will of the Divine and receive the support on their path that is possible; one has to simply ask.

I would remind you at this point that there are multitudes of beings in the heavenly realms who will support you; you need only ask. The Divine has provided you with a Guardian Angel, with guides and a channel to your soul in order that you can align with the will of the soul and the will of the Divine.

Many forget these avenues of support, and I would encourage you to use all the support that is available to you.

The Flame of Miracle will support the manifestation of your highest intention, for indeed a miracle is simply an act that is of the highest intention for the highest good of all.

ALL THAT THERE IS

Your perception of the word miracle may need to be adjusted, dear soul. Remember who you truly are. You are a Divine being. As such you have access to all of the support that this Universe provides so that you can create miracles every day.

You simply need to focus your intention, focus your will for the highest good of all and, if in accordance with the will of the Divine, it shall be so!

"….Sisters and brothers, brothers and sisters, you are ONE…."

**The Archangelic Collective The Seraphim
Channelled by Angela Orora Medway-Smith**
The Book of Many Colours, April 2021

The Flame of Healing
The 22nd Ray
The Ray of Healing

Patron: The Archangel Raphael
Colour: Sky Blue
Symbol: The Caduceus

Properties: Communication, expression, creativity, the herald, the messenger. Writing, art, drama, communication, technology. Healing, sacred sound, song, mantra, chant. Travel and protection when travelling, navigation and discovery. The air element and elementals (sylphs, borreas, aura etc), telepathy, and mediumship.

Invocation:

Creator, I AM spirit bright
Round me burn your flame of light
From Archangelic Flame
Called forth now in your name
I invoke the Flame of Healing
Guarded and guided by Archangel Raphael
To (insert your intention here)
With pure intent for the highest outcome and harm of none
In accordance with your will and the Divine plan

The Archangel Raphael speaks:

I am Raphael, an Angel of Creation, Angelic Patron of the 22nd Divine Ray and I oversee and am Guardian of the Sacred Flame of Healing. The Flame of Healing is being employed by many lightworkers.

The past one hundred years have seen the channelling of many different healing modalities which tap into aspects of The Flame of Healing; each of these differing vibrations is suitable for different individuals. They, although having the same root, are different branches of the same tree, yielding different fruit.

SELF

Healing energy takes many forms. It is commonly found channelled by creative individuals who create music, art, sculpture, words that soothe the spirit and troubled soul. Do not disregard the power of such healing. Remember how your day can be brightened by the sight of a beautiful image or sound of some favourite tune.

At its finest vibration, the Flame of Healing can be used to support such creative individuals as well as to support those who are energy healers. Use the Flame of Healing for yourself in any way you feel guided.

Invoke my presence and I will support you. Call in and visualise my caduceus before you begin your writing practice, your music composition, your healing session and invoke my support and that of the Flame of Healing for the betterment of self and, as such, the raising of vibration for all.

OTHERS

For others, the Flame of Healing will primarily be employed as a boost, particularly for those healers who require additional support with their healing practice.

To many healers, I am an old friend, standing by your side in the delivery of healing energy for the highest good of all and harm of none.

Dearest one, if you are not familiar with my energy, bid me join you, invoke the Flame of Healing alongside the modality you channel and feel the difference.

ALL THAT THERE IS

Equally, the Flame of Healing can be invoked and deployed to support groups of individuals, to all sentient beings, to the lands, rivers, seas, oceans and waterways, to the plant Kingdom, to all that there is.

Feel my presence support you, dearest one, invoke the energy of the Flame of Healing for All that there is; you will be surprised what can be achieved with intention!

The Flame of Life
The 30th Ray
The Ray of Earth Consciousness

Patron: Cosmic Ascended Master Sanat Kumara

Colour: Deep Red

Symbol: Earth Square (Tatwas)

Properties: The bridge to the consciousness of the Earth Spirit Gaia, the High Priest of the Earth Spirit, her ambassador, and translator. All devas and elementals (gnomes, mountain devas, dryads, and plant devas etc) the mineral, vegetable kingdom and animal kingdoms. Earth healing, the energy system of the Earth.

Invocation:

Creator, I AM spirit bright

Round me burn your flame of light

From Cosmic Ascended Master Flame

Called forth now in your name

I invoke the Flame of Life

Guarded and guided by Sanat Kumara

To (insert your intention here)

With pure intent for the highest outcome and harm of none

In accordance with your will and the Divine plan

The Cosmic Ascended Master Sanat Kumara speaks:

Ah! You have heard my call, dearest one!

I am Sanat Kumara and I encourage you to invoke the Flame of Life to support your beloved Gaia, to support her healing and the healing of her inhabitants, not simply humankind.

SELF

Call upon the Flame of Life when you wish to both commune with and send healing energy to the other inhabitants of your planet, Gaia, Patchamama, the Earth, YOUR mother.

OTHERS

You may intend this Flame, this energy, for others when you wish that they be better connected to the many that inhabit the earth alongside you.

You may decide to invoke the Flame of Life and intend that your leaders be inspired to consider others than themselves or humankind in their endeavours and of course you may invoke other Sacred Flames alongside the Flame of Life to support these endeavours.

ALL THAT THERE IS

Clearly, your intention for healing for the different beings who live on your planet alongside you would be the focus of your intention here.

Sit within the sacred symbol, invoke the Sacred Flame and use the web of life, the flower of life, the energy of the Flame of Interconnectedness to intend such healing energy be channelled to different kingdoms and indeed through the energy system of your beloved Gaia.

Invoke my presence and I will support you.

*"….This Ray, this energy, affects a contemplative state beloved.
You are all capable of reaching such a state.
Discipline, dedication and trust are required of the disciple who awaits guidance from the Divine…."*

The Cosmic Ascended Master Lord Kahn
Channelled by Angela Orora Medway-Smith
The Book of Many Colours, April 2021

The Flame of Justice
The 33rd Ray
The Ray of Protection

Patron: The Archangel Michael
Colour: Electric Blue
Symbol: The Sword

Properties: Protection, perception and passion, transformation, alchemy, and courage. The warrior of light, spiritual rescue (psychopomp work), entity release, spiritual clearing. The spiritual warrior, motivation, justice, harmony, and Karma. Sensuality, sexuality and attraction, justice, right action, and harmony.

Invocation:

Creator, I AM spirit bright

Round me burn your flame of light

From Archangelic Flame

Called forth now in your name

I invoke the Flame of Justice

Guarded and guided by Archangel Michael

To (insert your intention here)

With pure intent for the highest outcome and harm of none

In accordance with your will and the Divine plan

The Archangel Michael speaks:

I am Michael, bearer of the Sword of Justice, Guardian of the Ray of Protection and the Flame of Justice; there are many things that can be achieved by one who seeks to work with me.

SELF

Protection. For thousands of years, mankind has understood my role as protector serving mankind on behalf of the Divine. An individual may request support at any time with protection, to seek justice, to bring courage and positive transformation. I may also assist with the clearing of unnecessary energies or entities that have entered the space of the individual.

OTHERS

Ask and it shall be so, call on the Flame of Justice when you seek to repatriate earthbound souls. I can be of great support with this endeavour. Work with, invoke my brother the Archangel Azrael and the Flame of the Akasha in alignment with me during this task.

One may also refer to the occasions detailed previously and utilise those for the benefit of others.

My light, my love, this Sacred Flame will support you in your endeavours. Be not afraid to tackle those energies that bring fear to your heart and belly.

Understand when you invoke my energy, I stand with you, beside you, supporting you in your endeavours.

ALL THAT THERE IS

Using your intuition as to the greatest benefit that you can provide to All that that there is, is recommended.

The Flame of Justice brings courage, perception, justice, right action and harmony, transformation and alchemy; invoking the Flame of Justice and requesting that this energy be transmitted to All that there is maybe a way that you would like to consider.

Clearly invoking the energy of the Seraphim or the Cherubim, spreading your intention for the Flame of Justice in alignment with the Flame of Divine Love For All and in alignment with the Flame of Universal Consciousness would be an excellent possibility for invocation of this Sacred Flame.

"...Should you, dearest one, wish to lead, call me for support, call me for guidance, call me to support your wisdom, call me to lead with dignity and integrity and in the highest good of all."

The Cosmic Ascended Master Moses
Channelled by Angela Orora Medway-Smith
The Book of Many Colours, **April 2021**

The Flame of Accord
The 40th Ray
The Ray of Law

Patron: Cosmic Ascended Master Moses
Colour: Blue Grey
Symbol: The Crook (The Herald's Staff)

Properties: Universal Law, order, harmony, truth, faith, belief. Divine order, the Divine plan, esoteric mechanics, the Spiritual Laws. Guidance, leading by example, the living of the spiritual life, the spiritual path. Hope, inspiration, miracle and magic, salvation, escape, the leader and advocate.

Invocation:

Creator, I AM spirit bright
Round me burn your flame of light
From Cosmic Ascended Master Flame
Called forth now in your name
I invoke the Flame of Accord
Guarded and guided by Moses
To (insert your intention here)
With pure intent for the highest outcome and harm of none
In accordance with your will and the Divine plan

The Cosmic Ascended Master Moses speaks:

What am I to say to you, beloved, about the Flame of Accord? It is what it says! This is the Sacred Flame that weaves through the Universe supporting the enabling of the spiritual laws.

SELF

Beloved, consult and invoke the Flame of Accord when you wish to align with the laws of our Universe; when you wish for support in creating harmony for the self that is based on external factors.

Using this Flame for Self brings benefit to all, for as the individual allies with the spiritual laws, becoming 'in flow' rather than swimming against the current, the benefit to all will be felt through the increased vibration of that individual.

OTHERS

Call upon this Sacred Flame to support the building of relationships both for Self and for others.

Always being mindful of invoking healing and this energy for the highest good of all.

You might consider intending this energy to support your leaders, conjoining this Flame with the Flame of Unity.

This, indeed, will have great impact on decisions made by your politicians. Consider supporting them in this way.

ALL THAT THERE IS

Invoking the Flame of Accord and applying its energy to all that there is, is obviously clearly beneficial.

To be of service you may wish to invoke the Flame of Grace, the Flame of Unity, or other of the Sacred Flames that you feel so drawn to in order to have a positive effect on all that there is.

Intend this energy for entire countries if you do so feel, continents, as well as the planet herself, if you are drawn to do so.

*"Beloveds, to some of you I am an old friend.
Others not acquainted with my energy
I bid you welcome.
You will come to know and regard me as friend and
ally..."*

The Archangel Raphael

Channelled by Angela Orora Medway-Smith

The Book of Many Colours, April 2021

The Flame of Life
The 44th Ray
The Ray of Birth

Patron: The Archangel Gabriel

Colour: Aquamarine

Symbol: The Chalice

Properties: Dreams, the Moon, messages and messengers, flow, grace, cleansing and synchronicity. Intuition, visions, clairvoyance and psychism. The astral planes and astral travel, magical manifestation. Sacred sound and resurrection. The water element and elementals (undine, naiad, nix, nereid and oceanid), the unconscious mind, and its powers!

Invocation:

Creator, I AM spirit bright
Round me burn your flame of light
From Archangelic Flame
Called forth now in your name
I invoke the Flame of Life
Guarded and guided by Archangel Gabriel
To (insert your intention here)
With pure intent for the highest outcome and harm of none
In accordance with your will and the Divine plan

The Archangel Gabriel speaks:

I am Gabriel, Angel of Creation, Angel of the Moon and waters. I am Patron of the Ray of Birth and Guardian of the Flame of Life.

All human life begins in the chalice.

SELF

Beloved there are many, many reasons that you might call upon my energy; I can support you with many things. In my capacity as Patron of the Ray of Birth, my tasks are more focused.

You may summon me for assistance with all forms of communication; including those with beings other than your kind.

If you wish to understand your dreams better, your unconscious mind better, you would do well to do so under my Patronage; with this and many things I can support you.

OTHERS

Call upon the Flame of Life to support those who give birth, as in all things ensuring that the healing you request is provided for the highest good of all, in accordance with the will of the Divine.

You may invoke the Flame of Life to support others in all forms of communication with all beings; not simply those who inhabit physical bodies.

ALL THAT THERE IS

Beloved, you may invoke my presence, request that this energy supports those in better communication with beings on all levels - working with my brothers and sisters the Seraphim - intending the sending of this Sacred Flame and perhaps or availing yourself of other mechanisms to intend this energy for the benefit of All that there is.

Be creative, dearest one, use this sacred energy for the betterment of all without fear, for I stand by your side when you do so, with love.

"Beloveds, time is a human construct. Should you invoke the energy of this Ray it will become apparent that all is not as it seems..."

The Archangelic Collective The Elohim
Channelled by Angela Orora Medway-Smith
The Book of Many Colours, **August 2020**

The Flame of Wisdom
The 50th Ray
The Ray of Wisdom

Patron: The Cosmic Ascended Master Solomon

Colour: Gold

Symbol: A Golden Ring (to wear upon the finger)

Properties: Wisdom, wisdom in action, spiritual leadership, rulership, and command. Esoteric and spiritual knowledge and truth, the intellect in combination with intuition, comprehension, spiritual and magical laws, and spiritual mechanics. Angelic communion and magic, the Merkabah and dimensional travel.

Invocation:

Creator, I AM spirit bright

Round me burn your flame of light

From Cosmic Ascended Master Flame

Called forth now in your name

I invoke the Flame of Wisdom

Guarded and guided by Solomon

To (insert your intention here)

With pure intent for the highest outcome and harm of none

In accordance with your will and the Divine plan

The Cosmic Ascended Master Solomon speaks:

Oh, the Flame of Wisdom is always present in your world! Its energy inspires and enlightens all, not simply those who seek.

SELF

The seeker should consider invoking the Flame of Wisdom both for their own spiritual development, personal development and well-being.

Wisdom is all. Information without wisdom is pointless. Actions taken without wisdom are potentially harmful.

Dearest one, invoke my presence, invoke the Flame of Wisdom when you wish assistance with guidance, choice, and ultimately action.

OTHERS

You may invoke the Flame of Wisdom and request my support when you consider that the leaders in your community, country or world require support.

If your request is in alignment with the will of the Divine then be assured that the Flame of Wisdom will sweep through those halls and offices where leaders control the destiny of the peoples.

Be also advised to send the Flame of Wisdom upwards in the ultimate chain of command to those who control the leaders of your peoples; for some are puppets, not acting in the best interests of their community and but dancing to the tune of others.

ALL THAT THERE IS

Dearest one, consider using the Flame of Wisdom in alignment with the Flame of Universal Consciousness sending it through the flower of life to reach all of those leaders (and their masters) who are in control of your domain.

As always, if this request is in alignment with the will of the Divine then it shall be so. Do not underestimate the power of this Flame, dearest one. Great changes, great advancements, can be manifested for your planet and ultimately for the benefit of all.

"….It is important to be careful not to influence free will as one does not wish to fall foul of the Laws of Karma. However, do not allow this fact to present you from asking or invoking a change for the highest good of all…."

The Cosmic Ascended Maha Cohan
Channelled by Angela Orora Medway-Smith
The Book of Many Colours, **August 2020**

The Flame of The Akasha
The 55th Ray
The Ray of Endings and Beginnings

Patron: The Archangel Azrael
Colour: Black
Symbol: The Scythe

Properties: Death and rebirth, incarnation, the Akashic Records, past lives, Karma, karmic cleansing, tie cutting and healing. Remembrance and restoration, the quintessential spiritual force of life, the Void. Time and cycles, inner light, creation, the progenitor, mystery, and magic. The Akashic element and elementals.

Invocation:

Creator, I AM spirit bright
Round me burn your flame of light
From Archangelic Flame
Called forth now in your name
I invoke the Flame of the Akasha
Guarded and guided by Archangel Azrael
To (insert your intention here)
With pure intent for the highest outcome and harm of none
In accordance with your will and the Divine plan

The Archangel Azrael speaks:

I am the Archangel Azrael, Patron of the 55th Ray, the Ray of Endings and Beginnings and Guardian of the Flame of the Akasha.

SELF

You may seek my assistance for yourself. I will accompany you to the Halls of the Akasha, wherein lies the key to your past, the record of previous incarnations of your soul.

Seeking this information for self can bring healing, healing that will then flow through forward generations so that your progeny are not limited by your actions. So that information and guidance can be yours on past lives, past trauma and, in short, past events that have an impact on your current and future path; not simply in this life but in any life that follows and the time between lives.

OTHERS

You may seek my support to invoke the energy of this Flame when you seek to travel to the Halls of the Akasha to support others with their quest for healing in this life.

You may also seek my assistance in supporting those you love or those you work with who near the end of their human life; in this way they will become accustomed to my energy and when the time comes for them to travel onward, their journey can be less disharmonious.

ALL THAT THERE IS

At times of great disaster and the death of many, I am present in my capacity as wayshower; the guides, guardians and departed loved ones of those who travel onward at this time will assist in the return of spirits.

However, for some, their passing comes as a shock. Some do not feel ready to leave this world at this time and are too attached either to individuals or worldly things.

Should you wish to assist such earthbound spirits returning to their souls in their transition, you may call me to support you in this work.

Equally, should you be part of a group that wishes to support the so-called rescue of earthbound souls, my presence and The Flame of the Akasha can be summoned to smooth the way.

Be not afraid to invoke this energy; your rewards will be great.

Additionally, you may summon the Flame of the Akasha to assist in cutting energetic ties, for transmuting karma, and supporting others with their souls' path in this way.

Sisters and brothers, my role is to support you, the Flame of the Akasha is a powerful ally. Fear not, if your will, your intention is aligned with a soul's path, sent with the highest intention and for the highest good of all and harm of none, support will be provided.

I have had somewhat of a bad press and am feared by some. Beloved soul, invoke my energy and feel for yourself!

The Flame of Receptivity
The 60th Ray
The Ray of the Priestess

Patron: Cosmic Lady Ascended Master Isis

Colour: Malachite Green

Symbol: The Crescent Moon

Properties: The Divine Feminine, wisdom power and magic; the magic and wisdom of the Moon. Motherhood, nurture, protection and healing, the mother's love. The power of the wife, the healer, resurrection, foresight, prophecy, oracle, silence, and stillness.

Invocation:

Creator, I AM spirit bright

Round me burn your flame of light

From Cosmic Ascended Master Flame

Called forth now in your name

I invoke the Flame of Receptivity

Guarded and guided by Isis

To (insert your intention here)

With pure intent for the highest outcome and harm of none

In accordance with your will and the Divine plan

The Cosmic Lady Ascended Master Isis speaks:

Sisters and brothers, many of you will remember life spent in service in my temples. Those drawn to working with the Flame of Receptivity will be souls who are healers.

Remember who you are, dearest one!

SELF

Sit in stillness.

Invoke the Flame of Receptivity.

Open your mind, open your heart, bathe your spirit in stillness; in this space, guidance, information and knowledge from your soul and the Divine will flow. Invoke my presence and I will support with you.

OTHERS

Similarly, you may enter this sacred space within the Ray of the Priestess and invoke the Flame of Receptivity to be of service to others.

Whether you are healer, oracle or simply mother, wife, parent or loving guide, guidance and healing will be forthcoming if you work for the highest good of those you serve.

ALL THAT THERE IS

Remember the power of your Moon.

Invoking the Flame of Receptivity for large groups of individuals, that they might be guided by the Divine for the highest good of all might be achieved more readily when working within the Moon's cycles.

Understand what can be achieved in this respect wisdom, not simply the wisdom of the Flame of Wisdom as patronised by my brother Solomon, but sacred wisdom of the Divine Mother, the Divine Feminine.

You may choose to invoke both these Sacred Flames together to assist your leaders.

Your service in this matter will be greatly rewarded.

"…The healing energy of this Ray is akin to water that falls lightly like rain but also in huge waves and torrents as a tsunami.
The feminine energy that this Ray represents is being rebalanced at this time.
Balance will return…"

The Ascended Master Lady Nada

(The Magdalene)

Channelled by Angela Orora Medway-Smith

The Book of Many Colours, **April 2021**

The Flame of Cosmic Love
The 66th Ray
The Ray of Unconditional Love

Patron: The Archangel Haniel
Colour: Kunzite Pink
Symbol: The Heart

Properties: Unconditional love, the awakening of the Higher Heart, compassion, mercy, love and empathy. The way and wisdom of the Divine Mother, forgiveness, absolution, repentance (as in turning towards the Divine). Connection to the tapestry of life, animal communication, emotional healing.

Invocation:

Creator, I AM spirit bright
Round me burn your flame of light
From Archangelic Flame
Called forth now in your name
I invoke the Flame of Cosmic Love
Guarded and guided by Archangel Haniel
To (insert your intention here)
With pure intent for the highest outcome and harm of none
In accordance with your will and the Divine plan

The Archangel Haniel speaks:

In simple terms, beloved, all is love and love is all; love is everywhere. It permeates the very fabric of existence, catches even the individual with the most hardened heart unawares.

I, Haniel, am Patron of the Ray of Unconditional Love, Guardian of the Flame of Cosmic Love.

SELF

The most profound beneficial reason for invoking the Flame of Cosmic Love is to invoke that love for oneself, awakening the energy point (chakra) that is dormant for many, the Higher Heart. Once awakened, the true essence of the soul will shine! Sometimes blindingly!

Those who knew you before this awakening will wonder what has changed; as you channel cosmic love, your personal vibration increases, as does the potential for your soul's ascension.

Repent misdeeds in this love, deal with those issues of karma that hinder your ascension, bring them to me, dearest one, and I will walk with you.

OTHERS

Oh, beloved! The joy, the healing, the love you can spread when you intend this energy for others! BE LOVE, SHINE LOVE, call on my support, and I will stand by you willingly!

ALL THAT THERE IS

Beloved, conjoin the Flame of Cosmic Love with that of other Sacred Flames, as you are so inspired, request support from their Patrons and acting in love for all, for the highest good, intend this energy where you will!

Should you wish to be of service to those of light, the invocation of this Sacred Flame is a worthy, worthy task to be undertaken with great joy!

"....Connect with me to remember your place in this world, to remember your connectedness to all that there is and to remember your true self."

The Ascended Master Kuthumi
Channelled by Angela Orora Medway-Smith
The Book of Many Colours, April 2021

The Flame of True Magic
The 70th Ray
The Ray of Magic

Patron: The Cosmic Ascended Master Merlin

Colour: The Dark Rainbow (Labradorite)

Symbol: The Wand

Properties: Magic, arcane wisdom, magical law and truth, magical correspondence. Service, knowledge, intelligence, and comprehension. The impossible and improbable – the cosmic trickster, initiator, and challenger – rites of passage. Sight and vision, prophecy, divination, fortune and destiny!

Invocation:

Creator, I AM spirit bright

Round me burn your flame of light

From Cosmic Ascended Master Flame

Called forth now in your name

I invoke the Flame of True Magic

Guarded and guided by The Merlin

To (insert your intention here*)

With pure intent for the highest outcome and harm of none

In accordance with your will and the Divine plan

*please read the channelled message first!

The Cosmic Ascended Master Merlin speaks:

Ah, we meet again!

The Flame of True Magic is not one that can be used lightly for it is powerful beyond your comprehension, dear child.

Many of you employ magic, which is, in your understanding, a method of manifestation; you would be wise to consider all of the karmic ramifications of such actions.

SELF

Dear child, I can assist you in developing your understanding of true magic. Be very aware of its power, be ultimately aware of its impact, not just on the self but on All that there is; for when you tap into the Flame of True Magic, all is possible.

I bid you to employ foresight and great care before employing this Sacred Flame.

OTHERS

Understand, dear child, that when you invoke the Ray, the Flame of True Magic, to influence the path of others, spend time considering the ramifications of this action.

You also need to understand that invocation of this Sacred Flame, of this Divine Ray, MUST ally with the will of the Divine and the will of the higher Self.

I cannot stress this importance!

ALL THAT THERE IS

Child, read the words above once more, continue to read them; you need to understand the power of the Flame of True Magic before you make any move to connect with this energy.

Always focus on the impact of your actions on All that there is.

You MUST act in Accordance with the will of the Divine otherwise, the karmic implications of your actions will resound for millennia.

Behave responsibly!

"…Perfect peace is possible within the vibration of this Ray. Go within dearest ones, go within. Listen to what your heart speaks, go within. Listen to what your soul speaks, go within. Listen to the Divine speak…"

The Ascended Lady Master Mary
Channelled by Angela Orora Medway-Smith
The Book of Many Colours, **April 2021**

The Flame of Ascension
The 77th Ray
The Ray of Evolution

Patron: The Archangel Samael
Colour: Blood Red
Symbol: The World Tree (The Tree of Life)

Properties: Change, evolution, ascension, movement, impermanence, growth, cycle, expansion, unfoldment. The 12-strand DNA, the Tree of Life, the Celtic World Tree – the Anima Mundi – the spine of the world. Motivation, passion, criticism, perspective, and opinion. Challenger and those who trigger others. The shadow self, sacrifice.

Invocation:

Creator, I AM spirit bright

Round me burn your flame of light

From Archangelic Flame

Called forth now in your name

I invoke the Flame of Ascension

Guarded and guided by Archangel Samael

To (insert your intention here)

With pure intent for the highest outcome and harm of none

In accordance with your will and the Divine plan

The Archangel Samael speaks:

I am Samael. I am an Angel of the Violet Flame; however I am also the Patron of the Ray of Evolution and as such the Guardian of the Flame of Ascension.

SELF

If you are serious about your own Ascension, beloved, invoke this energy! It is not, as you say, rocket science!

You, as an individual soul, are constantly evolving. You can bring in focus on this path by calling in the Flame of Ascension to support you with your own personal ascension.

You can call the Flame of Ascension to support you to seek and follow alternative pathways, transitions and all forms of growth.

It is no surprise that the tree of life is the symbol of this Ray. The Flame of Ascension can be of great support to you in a number of ways.

Should you find that you are challenged by the acts or energies of others, you may invoke the Flame of Ascension to guard you from the disharmonious effects on your person, on your psyche. All forms of change, evolution, growth, expansion and ascension may be supported by invoking this Flame.

OTHERS

You may intend, invoke and employ the Flame of Ascension for others to support them in the ways described above; it is not necessary to repeat myself.

ALL THAT THERE IS

Equally, you may invoke and employ the Flame of Ascension and intend its destination to be a group of individuals who you consider misinformed or the planet herself.

Invoking the Flame of Ascension around your Earth can only be for the betterment of mankind. As the vibrations on the planet ascend, those who align to this vibration will thrive, while those who are limited may choose to depart, attend to the spiritual growth in other dimensions and return when they are ready.

The cycle of birth, growth, maturity, death and decay is natural; the Flame of Ascension can assist to maximise the opportunity for growth in your time on this planet, and you would be well advised to employ it.

Guidance and support are yours when you invoke my presence, when you invoke the Flame of Ascension; be aware beloved of recognising the physical symptoms of Ascension, your physical body may take some time in aligning to your new vibration, and we the patrons have asked the medium to include such information in these pages for your support and enlightenment.

"...The Violet Flame, this ray of magic, transmutation and alchemy, can enable you to bring about great and sweeping changes in your life..."

The Ascended Master St Germain

Channelled by Angela Orora Medway-Smith

***The Book of Many Colours*, April 2021**

The Flame of Order
The 80th Ray
The Ray of Order

Patron: The Cosmic Ascended Master Lord Kahn

Colour: Diamond White

Symbol: The Blossoming Lotus

Properties: Harmony, peace, order, resolution, equilibrium, balance, calm. Stillness, the zero point. Restoration, realignment to the Divine and the spiritual path, the wayshower and herald; those who lead by example. Mediator and counsellor. The Ray of peacekeepers, healing, sanctuary, home and retreat.

Invocation:

Creator, I AM spirit bright

Round me burn your flame of light

From Cosmic Ascended Master Flame

Called forth now in your name

I invoke the Flame of Order

Guarded and guided by Lord Kahn

To (insert your intention here)

With pure intent for the highest outcome and harm of none

In accordance with your will and the Divine plan

The Cosmic Ascended Master Lord Kahn speaks:

I am Lord Kahn. I bring harmony and order.

SELF

The seeker who places him or herself in the care of the Flame of Order will be rewarded as follows; alignment and harmony in those areas of one's life, sanctuary, peace and resolution.

The Flame of Order restores perfect equilibrium. Harmony of this kind is difficult to achieve without the assistance of the Flame of Order, harmony of this kind is that which many of the spiritual seekers of the Buddhist faith call 'nirvana'.

OTHERS

Beloved child, you may invoke my presence and request my assistance and employ the Flame of Order for the benefit of others so that the states described previously can be achieved by them.

Be advised that your intention, whilst important, must always align with the will of the Divine and the will of the soul of the individual in question you seek to support.

ALL THAT THERE IS

Peace, perfect peace, karmic balance and equilibrium for all of mankind, for elementals and all sentient beings that inhabit the planet alongside you is possible.

Should you be guided, you may choose to invoke the Flame of Order and organise group or mass meditation with this intention.

This intention, if it aligns with the will of the Divine at the time in question, will assist All that there is in reaching this state or order.

Seekers of harmony, rest in the Flame of Order and experience perfect peace.

"...Call on me when you wish to elevate the vibration of a discourse, of a relationship and elevate it with the essence of peace and compassion..."

The Ascended Lady Master Kwan Yin
Channelled by Angela Orora Medway-Smith
The Book of Many Colours, April 2021

The Flame of Divine Love In All
The 88th Ray
The Ray of Commonality
(Divine Love)

Patron: The Archangelic Collective The Cherubim

Colour: Deep Pink

Symbol: The Flaming Heart

Properties: The tapestry of love, the connecting thread that binds all things together through the love of their creator. The first web of all, the fabric of the Universe, affinity through love, empathy, compassion, community, and commonality of feeling. Sympathy, charity and mercy, forgiveness and second chances.

Invocation:

Creator, I AM spirit bright

Round me burn your flame of light

From Archangelic Flame

Called forth now in your name

I invoke the Flame of Divine Love In All

Guarded and guided The Cherubim

To (insert your intention here)

With pure intent for the highest outcome and harm of none

In accordance with your will and the Divine plan

The Archangelic Collective The Cherubim speak:

Dearest Divine Soul, we are The Cherubim. We are responsible for spreading the love of the Divine throughout the universe. How then can you best employ the Flame of the Divine Love In All?

We will make some suggestions herein; however, it is for you to decide, dearest Divine Soul, spread this Divine love freely. Your race and your planet are in much need.

SELF

Very simply, meditate, relax into the web of energy that we oversee; see yourself suspended in the love of the Divine.

Rest here when you wish to be filled with the love of the Divine, rest here when you wish to be reacquainted with your divinity, with your individual purpose as a being of light.

Nurture your being in this energy of Divine love.

OTHERS

Similarly, invoke the Flame of Divine Love In All and intend that your intended be held, nurtured, filled with Divine love.

Invoke the Flame of Divine Love In All to enable your intended to know their place in this universe; this will support them both in everyday endeavours and in those that are aligned to their souls' purpose.

ALL THAT THERE IS

Beloved, dear Divine Soul, invoke this Flame. Send it freely through the web of interconnectivity. Align this intention with that of our brothers, The Seraphim. By so invoking both Flames simultaneously great works can be achieved, spreading Divine love to All that there is.

What joy you can bring, what love you can spread, what great works you can achieve, dearest Divine Soul. There are no limitations to this Divine love!

Remember you are a spark of the Divine made in the image of the Creator and as such have the divine right to both tap into for the Self and to invoke this Sacred Flame for the benefit of others and All that there is.

*"...Sit beneath the World Tree for support...
for a deeper understanding of evolution and change.
To understand what has gone before and what is to
come."*

The Archangel Samael
Channelled by Angela Orora Medway-Smith
The Book of Many Colours, April 2021

The Black Flame of The Void
The 90th Ray
The Ray of the Cosmic Divine Mother

Patron: The Cosmic Lady Ascended Master Annami

Colour: Deep Blue Black

Symbol: The Black Rose

Properties: The Void, the beginning of all, chaotic ocean of infinite potential, the impossible chaos. Priestess of the Great Cosmic Mother. Dreaming and communion through dreams. Original magic and creation, healing the Soul, transcendence of Universal Law and limitation. Silence and absence and stillness.

Invocation:

Creator, I AM spirit bright

Round me burn your flame of light

From Cosmic Ascended Master Flame

Called forth now in your name

I invoke the Black Flame of The Void

Guarded and guided by Lady Annami

To (insert your intention here)

With pure intent for the highest outcome and harm of none

In accordance with your will and the Divine plan

The Cosmic Lady Ascended Master Annami speaks:

The Void, the Crucible of Creation, this beloved is not a place to be feared but a space in which you may achieve perfect rest.

SELF

Dear Soul, the Black Flame of the Void brings with it all possibilities.

Healing for the soul when necessary transcendence of universal and spiritual laws. For some, the Void feels like home; for others, an alien place. Do not fear the silence.

OTHERS

Dearest Soul, you may guide others to find solace in the energy of the Void.

The Black Flame of the Void brings with it all possibilities for renewal, for regeneration; its power, its magnificence cannot be conveyed!

ALL THAT THERE IS

The Black Flame of the Void can assist those who commune through dreams.

You may consider aligning this energy with the Flames of Wisdom, with the Flames of Love with even perhaps the Flame of Accord; creating opportunities for those who require inspiration in their capacity as leaders.

Rest within the energy of the Black Flame of the Void; it is a place of infinite potential!

"...The Void is the primordial lake of creation. Travel to this space when you wish your soul to be healed..."

The Cosmic Ascended Master Annami
Channelled by Angela Orora Medway-Smith
***The Book of Many Colours*, August 2020**

The Flame of Universal Consciousness
The 99th Ray
The Ray of Interconnection

Patron: The Archangelic Collective The Seraphim

Colour: Pale Champagne Gold

Symbol: The Flower of Life

Properties: The tapestry of life, the connecting thread that binds all things together through commonality of origin; the Divine. The second web of all, the fabric of the Universe, interconnection, alignment, the spiritual path and synchronicity. Communion and higher vibrational mediumship, shamanic unity consciousness.

Invocation:

Creator, I AM spirit bright

Round me burn your flame of light

From Archangelic Flame

Called forth now in your name

I invoke the Flame of Universal Consciousness

Guarded and guided by The Seraphim

To (insert your intention here)

With pure intent for the highest outcome and harm of none

In accordance with your will and the Divine plan

The Archangelic Collective The Seraphim speak:

We, The Seraphim, are responsible for the web of interconnection in this universe that bears many names. We are patrons of the Ray of Interconnection and Guardians of the Flame of Universal Consciousness. You are one.

SELF

You may invoke the Flame of Universal Consciousness when you wish to feel aligned with All that there is. You can similarly use this practice to receive energy from this web of life.

Invoking the Flame of Universal Consciousness and basking in its fire will remind you that you are one with All that there is.

Be reminded, dear child, that every thought you have, every deed, action, every manifestation that you create affects the consciousness of All that there is.

Be mindful, therefore, of your actions, deeds and thoughts of the smallest intentions, plans, hopes and dreams. Be aware of the karmic ramifications of self-indulgence, of greed, of being the purveyor of negativity.

OTHERS

You may invoke the Flame of Universal Consciousness to transmit information and healing energy to both individuals, groups and All that there is.

Be mindful of your intentions in these actions. Be mindful of the plan of the Divine; we will support you in your endeavours if your intention is aligned with the highest good of all and the will of the Divine.

ALL THAT THERE IS

We speak not only about the planet that you exist on; we speak of the Universe in its entirety when we speak of All that there is.

Visualise your place in the flower of life, feel our support, our energy, which can help assist you to rise above difficulty and challenge.

*We will support you with the invocation of the Flame of Universal Consciousness when invoked as we directed above to assist not only mankind, all sentient beings and your planet, but will have a positive effect on **ALL** that there is.*

"....Connect with this Ray when you wish to experience communion with the Creator of All. A merging of your energy with the Divine..."

The Cosmic Ascended Master The Maitreya
Channelled by Angela Orora Medway-Smith
The Book of Many Colours, April 2021

The Flame of Cosmic Time
The 100th Ray
The Ray of Time

Patron: The Archangelic Collective The Elohim

Colour: Lepidolite Blue (Glittering Pale Blue)

Symbol: The Infinity Loop (Lemniscate)

Properties: Time, infinity, cosmic time, timelessness, time travel. The qualities of time, love, grace, mercy – precognition and retrocognition – time suspension, bloating time, shrinking time. History remembered and lost, the mystery of the beginning (and ending) of all. The constraint of miracle and the working of miracle.

Invocation:

Creator, I AM spirit bright

Round me burn your flame of light

From Archangelic Flame

Called forth now in your name

I invoke the Flame of Cosmic Time

Guarded and guided by The Elohim

To (insert your intention here)

With pure intent for the highest outcome and harm of none

In accordance with your will and the Divine plan

The Archangelic Collective the Elohim speak:

Children of Gaia, understand that time is a human constraint, understand that there are many realities, many dimensions, where your time does not exist.

SELF

We are The Elohim. Call upon us to influence the cycle of your time. To expand the time that is available to you. If your request is in earnest and aligns with the will of the Divine, then it shall be so.

Much can be achieved when your time is expanded. Consider this, consider how you will use such infinite time. Will you use it for the betterment of all? Will you use it for the betterment of Self only? Recognise and understand the implications of your choices.

OTHERS

Should your intention be the expansion of time in order to support the healing, betterment, ascension of others then in all likelihood if your request meets with the will of the Divine it will be acceded. Be ever mindful, dear child, of the root of your intention.

ALL THAT THERE IS

Calling first on the Flame of Cosmic Time and our support, then invoking perhaps the Flame of Order would be of great benefit to All that there is.

There are many possibilities in which you can use the Flame of Cosmic Time for the betterment of All that there is.

Ponder, dearest one, gather those souls around you who wish to drive such changes; channel such healing energies, perhaps?

Focus first on expanding the time available to you for this work and using this time most wisely for the benefit of All that there is.

This Flame is perhaps your most powerful tool, used first with the addition of invocation of other Patrons and Sacred Flames there are infinite possibilities.

The Magdalene Flame

I would like to go into more depth about the Magdalene Flame. The original channellings from spirit regarding this Sacred Flame came from Edwin Courtenay many years ago; the Masters have added more detail in the creation of this book.

Earlier in this section, the simple view of the Magdalene Flame is illustrated. In her channelling, Lady Nada explained that the Magdalene flame is multi-layered and talks about the different ways that you can connect with this energy.

You can choose to illuminate your being with the aspect of the Magdalene Flame that is the knowledge of the divine feminine, The Gnostic Goddess Sophia, the rose pink energy (detailed on page 48).

Alternatively, you can invoke the Magdalene Flame in ALL of its aspects. Spirit has been clear that those who decide to work with the Flame in all of its aspects will be supported; they say this energy is much needed at this time.

Here is the explanation of the individual elements of the Magdalene Flame. You don't need to know the full story of Lady Nada's life as Mary Magdalene in order to channel the phenomenal healing power of this Sacred Flame.

The Magdalene Flame constituents:

* **The Christos,
  The Flame of Divine Service (incorporating Divine Love and Divine Surrender)**
  (Ruby Red - Masculine)
  This is the masculine Christ energy, representative of passion, motivation, commitment and promise; the inherent knowledge of our destiny and divine purpose; why we are here and what we are meant to contribute to the Divine design. Mary Magdalene was initiated into this energy directly through her coupling with the Master Jesus who embodied this energy.

* **The Golden Ray of Christ, The Christ Healing Ray & Flame**
  (Gold - Masculine)
  The healing Ray of her son James; this energy, a specific manifestation of the Cosmic Christ's miraculous healing power, entered into Mary Magdalene when she was carrying James. James became the Saint who would become its representative on Earth. Mary Magdalene was initiated in this energy through the process of carrying the child.

* **The Sophia, The Flame of Divine Feminine Wisdom**
  (Rose Pink - Feminine)
  This is the feminine Christ energy; representative of the wisdom of the heart (not knowledge), which is inherited wisdom from our past lives, the intuitive wisdom from this lifetime, coupled with the wisdom of the Soul and the Divine that we have access to. This was the energy that Mary Magdalene carried, and had been initiated into, initially in the Hebrew Temple.

* **The Shekinah, Mother Mary, The Flame of Nurture**
  (Madonna Blue - Feminine)
  This is the power of the Divine Mother; the mother nurturing

energy that has the power to trigger internal healing through comfort, love and protection. This is the energy that Mary Magdalene was initiated into by the Mother Mary, who was herself a High Priestess of the Shekinah; it was the energy that Mary the Mother held and the Divine Ray which she is Patron of.

❀ The Maitreya, The Flame of Divine Order
(Clear pure white - the masculine and feminine flames of the Christ energy combined together as one)
This is the presence and power of the Maitreya, the cosmic Christ transcendent of duality and gender which was held by the Christ Child Sarah and which Mary Magdalene became initiated into when she carried Sarah. This is the power of returning home to the Divine through the guiding, steering, anchoring presence of the Christ, which is both within us, as part of our spirit, and outside of us as the Maitreya calling us home like a beacon.

❀ The Siege, The Black Flame of the Void
(Deep Blue Black - Feminine)
This is the power of the Divine Hag, the Black Madonna, the Veiled Isis. The progeny Goddess of the Void, the beginning and the end; the great silence of transcendent and absolute knowing. Like the Cosmic Christ energy, the energy of the Goddess Siege is transcendent of limitation and, in truth, gender; though she is seen as feminine because of her power of creation which here on Earth is seen as a feminine trait. Mary Magdalene adopts this energy in the final phase of her life when she becomes the widow, the grieving, mourning wife of the resurrected Christ, the personified goddess of silence who maintains invisibility for the sake of her daughter. The Patron of this Divine Ray is the Cosmic Lady Ascended Master Annami.

These manifestations of the Divine energy of the Christ and of the Goddess are then what humanity need now in order to navigate the trials and tribulations that they are experiencing personally and globally.

Invocation

Here is a sample invocation. Please remember to *insert* and *assert* your intention.

Creator, I AM spirit bright
Around me burn your flames of light
From the Sacred Divine Flames
Called forth now in your name
I invoke ALL aspects of the Magdalene Flame
Guarded and guided by the Patrons of Light
Form around me, a tube of power and light
to (insert your intention)
With pure intent for the highest outcome and harm of none
In accordance with your will and the Divine plan
And so it is (or Amen if you prefer)

From time to time, I run workshops specifically on working with the Magdalene Flame, which give much more information on the life of Mary, and I talk about my past life experience with Lady Nada in her incarnation as the Magdalene (*You can also find a healing meditation with the Magdalene Flame in the shop on my website,*)

The Threefold or Ascension Flame

No reference book on the Sacred Flames would be complete without a discussion of the Threefold or Ascension Flame.

You will have seen that the Patrons, through their channellings, widely encourage us to work with combinations of different Esoteric Fires.

There are many different Threefold Flames (or Ascension Flames) and an internet search will yield many different options, suggested by different spiritual bodies and teachers. The choice is yours!

It is up to you to exercise your discernment and follow your intuition, asking your guides which is the most relevant and useful combination of esoteric flames for you at this moment in time.

The Threefold Flame combination that the Patrons feel they want you to be aware of at this time consists of :

- The Magdalene Flame (Lady Nada and the 3rd Ray, pink)
- The Flame of Mastery (El Morya and the 4th Ray, royal blue)
- The Flame of Unification (Kuthumi, the 5th Ray, yellow)

You can use a simple visualisation to create an entwined flame by using the image on the cover of this book as a guide.

See the individual flames emanating separately from the Divine, becoming entwined together and then moving through a template of the flower of life that moves through your body or the body of the person for whom you intend this energy.

The invocation you use will be slightly different when you are calling in more than one Sacred Flame, and you might like to follow the template below or create your own as your own words carry more of a personal intention and are therefore more powerful.

(If you choose to work with different energies, simply replace the names of the Sacred Flames, the names of their Patrons, and give the reason for your invocation.)

Creator, I AM spirit bright
Around me burn your flames of light
From the Sacred Divine Flames
Called forth now in your name
I invoke thee, Flame of Love, Flame of Mastery, Flame of Unification
Guarded and guided by the Lady Nada, the El Morya
and Lord Kuthumi
Form around me, a tube of power and light to encourage and
promote my ascension and the ascension of the world
With pure intent for the highest outcome and harm of none
In accordance with your will and the Divine plan
And so it is (or Amen if you prefer)

Some spiritual teachings assert that the Threefold Flame resides in your heart/higher heart centre as a reflection of the same qualities of love, wisdom and power that manifests in the heart of the Divine, in the heart of your I AM presence and in the heart of your higher self; calling this divine spark your passport to immortality.

If that concept *feels right* to you, you can adopt it in visualisation, invoking the threefold flame from the divine and channelling it through the higher chakras to your heart and expanding it from there*. The choice is yours.

*A downloadable meditation is available from my website.

I shall leave you with another view of the Ascension Flame and a channelling from Aurelia Louise Jones where Adama of Telos speaks:

"This Flame contains the frequency and color of all the other Flames. You see or experience it as a brilliant, luminous, white dazzling light that consumes on contact all that is less than the perfection of Love. Its power and brilliance are limitless, sustaining worlds in perfect harmony and beauty.

Those invoking and working with it must prepare for change. Once touched by that Flame, you are never the same again. Everyone can work with it, of course, but in its full intensity, it holds the capacity to completely transform the initiate who has reached the doorway of Ascension.

When you are finally ready to take this leap in your evolution, you will be immersed in the frequency of that magnificent energy. It will propel you into the final step when the fires of Love will consume all human limitations, your full consciousness will be restored and all your bodies will align and unite.

You will then be invited to join the "immortals" as an ascended master. You will step into that glorious spiritual freedom and consciously reconnect with your Creator and with all that exists within His heart. This is, my friends, how powerful the Ascension Flame is."

Adama, channelled by Aurelia Louise Jones
The Ascension Flame of Purification and Immortality

Part Four

Seeking Support & Activating Allies

What things soever ye desire,

when ye pray

believe that ye receive them

and ye shall have them."

Mark 11:24

Support From Guides and Guardians

I'd like to share a little more about my personal spiritual journey with you. My faith in the Creator and my inner knowledge that we are all connected has been part of me for as long as I can remember.

As a child, I tuned into the guidance of my Guardian Angel and guides; at that age I didn't really understand the difference. I was in my early 20s when my *re-awakening* took place and my guides and guardians were able to step forward, speaking more clearly, much of the time but I did not pay as much attention to this guidance as I should!

Finally, in my 50s, I've learned to listen and act on the information that I'm being given; my connection to my guides, guardians, higher self and the beings of light from the Ascended Master and Archangelic Collective who support us all has become crystal clear.

Our higher self, guides and guardians will create opportunities for our learning when we need them, using whatever means available. Learning to listen and follow these signs, omens, portents and messages is *so* important.

When you do, your life will begin to flow with ease and grace and manifesting the life you dream of can become a reality.

This sounds too good to be true! I hear you thinking… But if you believe that, then it will be so!

To help you get started, I have recorded a downloadable meditation for you, during which you can connect to those guides and guardians who want to step forward to support you on your spiritual journey.

This is free to all who purchase this book and can be found as an MP3 download on my web page.

https://www.cariadspiritual.com/sacredflames

I also have a range of fully accredited courses in energy healing and intuitive and spiritual development available, crafted from the experience, knowledge and tools I've amassed in the past 35+years. These courses start with the fundamental knowledge you need before you embark on your spiritual path, to more complex esoteric teachings and energy healing attunements.

You can sign up to my newsletter here to receive notifications when new courses are added: https://www.cariadspiritual.com/

I wish you every blessing on your journey of discovery, of remembrance and spiritual growth.

You are a spark of the Divine; I hope that this journey will help you to remember the Divine Soul you truly are.

Allies From The Plant Kingdom

Plants, including trees, flowers, herbs and weeds, are probably our greatest allies. However, most of us take plants for granted. We assume because they do not have a brain that they are not sentient; science is now challenging that view and proving that is certainly not the case.

It was in 1880, over one hundred and forty years ago, that Charles Darwin in his book *The Power of Movement in Plants* first asked us to think of the plant as a kind of upside-down animal, with its main sensory organs and "brain" on the bottom, underground, and its sexual organs on top.

Since the 1980s, scientists in the field of plant neurobiology have conducted experiments which prove that plants have all the same senses as humans and more! *(The term neurobiology is something of a misnomer because even scientists in the field don't argue that plants have neurons or brains but instead have analogous structures.)*

Author Michael Pollan wrote an article for *The New Yorker* magazine about the developments in plant science called "The Intelligent Plant."

"They have analogous structures," Pollan explains. *"They have ways of taking all the sensory data they gather in their everyday lives ... integrate it and then behave in an appropriate way in response. And they do this without brains, which, in a way, is what's incredible about it, because we automatically assume you need a brain to process information."*

And we assume you need ears to hear. But researchers, says Pollan, have played a recording to plants of a caterpillar munching on a leaf and the plants react. They and their neighbours begin to secrete defensive chemicals even though the plant isn't really threatened, Pollan says, *"It is somehow hearing what is, to it, a terrifying sound of a caterpillar munching on its leaves".*

More information on scientific studies of plant behaviour can be found here: https://www.plantbehavior.org/resources/

Additionally, the BBC's documentary, *The Green Planet*, first broadcast in 2022, gives us visual proof of the intelligence of plants. https://www.bbc.co.uk/programmes/m0013cl7

Both these resources can open your eyes to the fascinating world of plants.

Vibrational Healing

This, and the preceding century have seen great advances in medicine and in the reintroduction of ancient medicine as complementary therapy. There have been countless academic studies and there is broad acceptance by scientists and the medical profession alike of the benefit of both ancient and modern vibrational medicine, from plants, colour, sound, crystal and pure energy vibration channelled by other human beings. Indeed, it was Albert Einstein that said:

> *"Future medicine will be the medicine of frequencies."*

In *The Book of Many Colours,* I introduce you to the concept of crystals as allies in any spiritual or healing work and give a comprehensive list of the crystals that align with each of the Divine Rays and Sacred Flames.

Here, the Patrons have asked me to point you in the direction of the allies you can find within the plant kingdom, suggesting ways that you might like to go about seeking more information; and perhaps, if you are so guided, experiment with some of the ancient healing methods derived from the plant kingdom that are available widely to you.

Plants are found on land, in oceans, and freshwater. They have been on Earth for millions of years.

For tens of thousands of years, mankind relied on the plant kingdom for sustenance, for medicine and for supporting life. We humans were foragers long before animal protein and farming changed our diets.

Allopathic medicine has made us less reliant on the plant kingdom, and for many, the food we eat is filled with manmade chemicals. Whilst the advances in modern medicine have meant that we as a species survive longer, our bodies are constantly challenged by chemicals that they were not designed to process.

At no point should any healer or complementary medicine practitioner tell you to disregard the advice of your doctor, or what to eat, and this is not what this chapter is about.

This chapter is not meant to be exhaustive; it is simply a starting point for you to begin an exploration into the allies in the plant kingdom who are there to support us.

Some of you may find the concept of honouring the plants that support and sustain us a strange concept. However, there has been much scientific research on this subject; in a study performed by the UK Royal Horticultural Society, researchers discovered that talking to your plants really can help them grow faster. Interestingly, they also found that plants grow faster to the sound of a female voice than to the sound of a male voice. Other studies have experimented with different sound levels and even the kinds of things that are said to plants and found that they actually do respond better to compliments rather than insults!

Plants As Food

We are what we eat. Simple words, but do we really understand their true meaning and actually think before putting food or drink into our bodies?

It is only sensible to eat the best quality food, to nurture and sustain our physical bodies. If your budget allows, then organic food might be an option that you might wish to consider.

Our ancestors gave thanks for all of the food they ate, blessing it as a matter of course. As a child growing up in the '60s this was also practised in many homes and schools. That has died out for the most part; you might wish to experiment with this idea.

Plants As Medicine

As mentioned earlier, for tens of thousands of years, mankind relied on the plant kingdom for sustenance, for medicine and for supporting life.

Generally, products made from botanicals or plants, that are used to treat diseases or to maintain health are called herbal products, botanical products, or phytomedicines. A product made from plants and used solely for internal use is called an herbal supplement. Plant medicine can be used topically (on the skin) or ingested by eating, drinking (or smoking).

Here are some of the most common forms of plant medicine. I've added them in alphabetical order and although I have tried and tested (and relied) on many of them over the last four decades, I do not give my opinion or share my experiences, as these are my personal perspectives.

The choice is yours, dear reader; you are the only person ultimately responsible for your own health, well-being, personal and spiritual development.

Australian Bush Flower Essences

Ian White is a fifth-generation Australian herbalist and the founder of Australian Bush Flower Essences; he is a BSc graduate from the University of NSW and has completed degrees in Naturopathy, Herbal Medicine, and Homeopathy.

The native plants of Australia have rare qualities and properties. This system, developed over a thirty-year period, captures their unique vibration and is designed for holistic healing.

Ayurveda

Ayurveda, a natural system of medicine, originated in India more than 3,000 years ago. The term *ayurveda* is derived from the Sanskrit words *ayur* (life) and *veda* (science or knowledge). Thus, Ayurveda translates to *knowledge of life*. It is based on the idea that disease is due to an imbalance or stress in a person's consciousness, Ayurveda encourages certain lifestyle interventions and natural therapies to regain a balance between the body, mind, spirit, and the environment.

Ayurveda treatment starts with an internal purification process, followed by a special diet, herbal remedies, massage therapy, yoga, and meditation. The concepts of universal interconnectedness, the body's constitution (*prakriti*) and life forces (*doshas*)) are the primary basis of ayurvedic medicine. Goals of the treatment aid the person by eliminating impurities, reducing symptoms, increasing resistance to disease, reducing worry, and increasing harmony in life.

Herbs and other plants, including oils and common spices, are used extensively in Ayurvedic treatment.

Bach Flower Remedies

Edward Bach studied medicine first in Birmingham and later at the University College Hospital, London, where he was House Surgeon. He also worked in private practice, having a set of consulting rooms in Harley Street, London. As a bacteriologist and pathologist, he undertook original research into vaccines in his own research laboratory.

There are 38 remedies in the Bach remedy system; all of them were discovered in the 1920s and 1930s by Dr Bach. Each remedy is associated with a basic human emotion. Mimulus, for example, is for when we are anxious or afraid about something specific. Taking the remedy is said to help overcome our fear and face it with courage. The remedies are in liquid form, preserved in brandy so that you can mix together the remedies you need to help balance your current emotional situation.

Essential Oils

Essential oils are basically plant extracts made by steaming or pressing various parts of a plant (flowers, bark, leaves or fruit) to capture the compounds that produce fragrance. It can take between several to hundreds of pounds of a plant to produce a single bottle of essential oil. There have been thousands of scientific studies conducted on their efficacy.

Aromatherapy, which has been used for centuries, is the practice of using essential oils for therapeutic benefit. When inhaled, the scent molecules in essential oils travel from the olfactory nerves directly to the brain and especially impact the amygdala, the emotional centre of the brain.

Essential oils can also be absorbed by the skin; a massage therapist might add a drop or two of wintergreen oil to help relax tight muscles during a rubdown, a skincare company may add lavender to bath salts to create a soothing soak.

Essential oils are widely available. It is important to remember that the vibrational quality of the essential oil you use will have an effect on the outcome of the therapy. Again, ensuring that the essential oil you use is created from plants that are ethically sourced and harvested and preferably grown organically. Generally, therapeutic grade essential oils will have the highest vibration.

Flower Essences, Waters and Extracts

Flower essences are water-based and made only from flowers. They are all-natural and help support healing through homeopathic means. This means that the flower essence is diluted many times over to reap the healing benefits (essential oils, on the other hand, are oil-based and made from the aromatic parts of plants).

Flower essences and essential oils are often confused with each other. Both solutions are made with plants but are prepared in very different ways.

Here's how flower essences are made:

- Flowers are submerged in natural spring water.
- The water is boiled or placed in the sun.
- The water is filtered and often preserved with brandy (eg *Bach Flower Remedies*). The finished essence contains no part of the flower.

Essences can be made with nonflowering plants and crystals using the same method. They can also be made without alcohol.

On the other hand, essential oils are concentrated liquids of plant compounds. Here's how they're made:

- The flowers, leaves, fruit, or bark of a plant are gathered. One bottle of essential oil often requires enormous quantities of plant material.
- The plant material is steamed, distilled or pressed, which extracts the fragrant compounds.
- The extracted "oil" is not actually oily and may be mixed with another "carrier oil" for use and preservation.

I remember making flower essences as a child, using rose petals. This is a fun activity you can do with children; you might also wish to teach children to speak kindly and ask the plant before removing the petals or better still wait for them to fall naturally. Clearly, the vibrational quality of all the material used is key. Using water from a sacred spring, a fresh running mountain spring rather than unfiltered tap water, for example, will have an effect on the final product.

Herbal Medicine

Our ancestors used plants as medicine for millennia and there are thousands of traditions worldwide.

When researching, I was interested to find that the World Health Organisation has been researching and documenting all of the plant medicine traditions of indigenous peoples around the world and this information is freely available on their website. Naturally, their views have a scientific slant, nevertheless, it is an invaluable resource for those interested in delving deeper into the world of plant medicine.

The simple traditions of our grandmothers, who created tinctures and poultices from the hedgerows, has been largely disregarded. I find it refreshing to see a resurgence in the interest in herbal medicine. After all, many common allopathic prescriptions have their original root in plant medicine before chemical synthesis replaced the humble plant!

Personally, my views on herbal medicine have been shaped by the results that have been achieved for myself and my family over the years.

Homeopathy

Homoeopathy is a complementary medicine based on a series of ideas developed in the 1790s by a German physician called Samuel Hahnemann.

A central principle of the treatment is that "like cures like", that a substance that causes certain symptoms can also help to remove those symptoms.

A second principle is based around the process of dilution and shaking called succussion. Practitioners believe that the more a substance is diluted in this way, the greater its power to treat symptoms.

Many homoeopathic remedies consist of substances that have been diluted many times in water until there's none, or almost none, of the original substance left.

Homoeopathy is used to treat an extremely wide range of conditions, including physical conditions such as asthma and psychological conditions such as depression. Many of you will be familiar with the commonly found homeopathic remedy, Arnica, which is used to support the body's healing after bruising.

Naturopathy

Naturopathic medicine is a system that uses natural remedies to help the body heal itself. It embraces many therapies, including herbs, massage, acupuncture, exercise, and nutritional counselling that has its roots in Germany in the 1800s, but some of its treatments are centuries old. Today, it combines traditional treatments with some aspects of modern science.

The goal of naturopathic medicine is to treat holistically, mind, body, and spirit. It also aims to heal the root causes of an illness, not just stop the symptoms. A naturopathic doctor may spend one to two hours examining you. They may ask questions about your health history, stress levels, habits and perhaps laboratory tests.

Afterwards, they will typically discuss your personal health plan. Naturopathic medicine focuses on education and prevention, so your doctor may give you diet, exercise, or stress management tips. They might use other complementary medicine modalities, like homeopathy, herbal medicine, and acupuncture, in addition to naturopathic treatments. They may also use touch, such as massage and pressure, to create balance in your body. This is called naturopathic manipulative therapy.

Many regulatory bodies exist for Naturopathic Practitioners, for example, in the United Kingdom. Naturopathic practitioners are registered with the Complementary National Health Council: https://www.cnhc.org.uk/

Nutritional Therapy

Nutritional therapy is the promotion of health through personalised nutrition and lifestyle support. It is a whole-body approach to nutrition and lifestyle medicine that addresses the potential underlying causes of ill-health rather than focusing on symptoms. Many nutritional therapists prescribe plant-based supplements.

Traditional Chinese Medicine

Western, or allopathic, medicine tends to view the body a lot like a car with its different operating systems that need the right inputs and outputs; it's very concrete and logical. Traditional Chinese Medicine, on the other hand, doesn't focus on science and medicine. Instead, it is based on balance, harmony, and energy. There are two central ideas behind it:

Qi: This is also called life energy or vital energy. The belief is that it runs throughout your body. It's always on the move and constantly changes. Traditional Chinese Medicine treatments often focus on ways to promote and maintain the flow of qi whether that is with acupuncture or herbal medicine.

Yin and Yang: These are opposites that describe the qualities of Qi.

- Yin: night, dark, cold, feminine, negative
- Yang: day, light, warm, positive, male

The belief is that everything in life has a little bit of its opposite, too, and balance is the key.

According to Traditional Chinese Medicine, these energies play out in our bodies. When you balance the yin and yang of qi, you feel healthy and well. If they're out of balance, you feel unwell. Traditional Chinese Medicine aims to create harmony and a healthy flow of qi.

Be aware that this system draws on the animal as well as the plant kingdom for the remedies prescribed by practitioners.

Plants Supporting Spiritual Development

For thousands of years, religious leaders and indigenous shamans have turned to the plant kingdom for support with spiritual development and spiritual practice.

Here is a short summary of some of the ways that the plant kingdom has supported us; again, this is not meant to be an exhaustive list, simply a sample of what resources are available to you.

Herbs/Resins

Herbs and plant extracts such as sage and palo santo are commonly used for cleansing/clearing energy. Resins, which have been created from plant extracts, are burned for the same purpose; frankincense and myrrh are still commonly used worldwide. This is a practice that has been used by mankind for centuries and is still continued today in churches and temples of many faiths, as well as by indigenous shamans and spiritual practitioners.

Please consider sustainability when using plant material for any of these methods, ensuring that the sage, palo santo or resin you burn is ethically farmed, harvested or produced; the vibration of the end product is inextricably linked to the planting, harvesting, processing etc.

In plant medicine ceremonies, plant material may be smoked or drunk. The facilitators should ensure the physical and emotional safety of all participants and create a safe physical environment. Their task also includes helping participants think about their intention or goal for the ceremony and helping participants integrate the lessons learned during the experience into their everyday lives.

Ultimately you are responsible for your part in this experience, it is your body, and any long term effects of these herbs should be considered before participating; as should the experience of your facilitator.

Sacred Oils

Sacred Oils are powerful tools for healing and expanding consciousness that form part of an ancient healing tradition that dates back thousands of years to the temples of Babylon, Egypt and beyond. They can be powerful tools for deep transformation, healing and consciousness and for working with the dying, for divination, prophecy and spiritual guidance.

Mention of sacred oils is found in the Old and New Testaments. The first mention of being Jacob in the book of Genesis and when Mosaic law was promulgated, the use of oil was prescribed for anointing priests, prophets, and kings, and the sacred vessels and vestments used in the service of religion. Sacred oils are still used by priests of many religions today.

Sacred oils can be used in meditation or the healing room in oil burners, diffusers or aura/space sprays. (There is a BIG difference in the vibrational energy of a sacred oil to that of an off-the-shelf essential oil; they may smell similar, but your experience and that of your client will be very different).

Myrrhophores, also known as myrrh-bearers or mistresses of the oils, were priestesses of an ancient order who worked with sacred oils to anoint those approaching death and to prepare the way for their soul to soar.

The sacred oil would realign people with their true soul essence and carry them to the *other side*. The myrrhophore would hold a vigil, usually for three days, whilst praying and uttering the intonation of the oil to heal the wounds in the soul caused by events not only in this life but also in the past. Mary Magdalene was a myrrhophore. Isis was a myrrhophore. Cleopatra, Hatshepsut, etc.

The myrrhophore not only works with dis-*ease* in the spirit and soul but also the disharmony within the environment. She tunes in to the subtle discordance and acknowledges its unrest. Turning to the oils, and its pure expression of the Divine, she offers herself as a bridge, bringing the gift of wholeness and healing.

In the Eastern Orthodox and Greek Catholic churches, the third Sunday of Pascha (ie, the second Sunday after Easter) is called the Sunday of the myrrh-bearers. During the time of Christ, being a myrrhophore was a very esteemed and honourable position. This myrrh-bearing tradition is kept alive today when we find Soul Midwives or Soul Doulas taking this role.

If you are interested in learning more, Felicity Warner's book *Sacred Oils* is an excellent starting point, and many teachers of Soul Midwifery can help guide you to blend sacred oils into your healing practice both for the living and the dying.

The Sacred Flames Alphabetically by Divine Ray

I am a lover of simplicity. I felt at this point it would be of great practical use to you to include a quick reference table.

I've organised this by the Divine Ray, very simply, think about the energy that you would like to bring forward, look for that in the Ray description and easily find the sacred flame, the Patron and other information.

I hope you find it helpful.

The Ray of	Active Principle	Patron	Ray	Crystal	Shape/Symbol	Colour
Accord	The Flame of Accord	Cosmic Ascended Master Moses	40	Lithium Quartz	The Crook	Blue Grey
Ascension	The Flame of Evolution	The Archangel Samael	77	Garnet	The World Tree	Blood Red
Birth	The Flame of Life	The Archangel Gabriel	44	Aquamarine	The Chalice	Aquamarine
Challenge	The Silver Violet Flame	The Lady Master Portia	9	Sugilite	Nonagon/Nonagram (9-Pointed Star)	Magenta
Commonality (Divine Love)	The Flame of Divine Love in All	The Archangelic Collective The Cherubim	88	Pink Sapphire	The Flaming Heart	Deep Pink
Cosmic Time	The Flame of Cosmic Time	The Archangelic Collective	100	Lepidolite	The Infinity Loop (Lemniscate)	Lepidolite Blue (Glittering Pale Blue)
Earth Consciousness	The Flame of Life	Cosmic Ascended Master Sanat Kumara	30	Red Jasper	Earth Square (Tatwas)	Deep Red
Endings Beginnings	The Flame of the Akasha	The Archangel Azrael	55	Hypersthene	The Scythe	Black
Grace	The Flame of Grace	Master Serapis Bey	2	Selenite	The Two Pillars	Selenite White

The Ray of	Active Principle	Patron	Ray	Crystal	Shape/Symbol	Colour
Harmony	The Flame of Compassion	The Masters Kwan Yin and Djwal Khul	8	Jade	Octagon/Octagram (Pointed Star)	Jade Green
Healing	The Flame of Healing	The Archangel Raphael	22	Blue Chalcedony	The Caduceus	Sky Blue
Interconnection	The Flame of Universal Consciousness	The Archangelic Collective The Seraphim	99	Seraphinite	The Flower of Life	Champagne Gold
Magic	The Flame of True Magic	The Cosmic Ascended Master Merlin	70	Labradorite	The Wand	The Dark Rainbow (Labradorite)
Miracle	The Flame of Miracle	Cosmic Ascended Master Maha Cohan	20	Blue Topaz	The Dove	Turquoise Blue
New Beginnings	The Magdalene Flame	The Lady Master Nada (Mary Magdalene)	3	Rose Quartz	Triangle	Rose Pink
Order	The Flame of Order	Cosmic Ascended Master Lord Kahn	80	Girasol Quartz	The Blossoming Lotus	Diamond White
Protection	The Flame of Justice	The Archangel Michael	33	Aqua Aura	The Sword	Electric Blue
Spiritual Alchemy	The Violet Flame	The Master St Germain	7	Amethyst	The Heptagon/ Heptagram (7-Pointed Star)	Violet
The Avatar	The Flame of Divine Service	Master Jesus/Sananda	1	Ruby	Single Pillar	Red

The Ray of	Active Principle	Patron	Ray	Crystal	Shape/Symbol	Colour
The Cosmic Divine Mother	The Black Flame of the Void	Cosmic Lady Ascended Master Annami	90	Jet	The Black Rose	Deep Blue Black
The Divine Father	The Flame of Divine Order	Cosmic Ascended Master Maitreya/ The Christ	10	Herkimer Diamond	The Sun	Pure White
The Divine Mother	The Flame of Nurture	Lady Master Mother Mary	6	Sodalite	Hexagon	Madonna Blue
The Green Ray	The Green Flame	The Archangel Uriel	11	Verdite	The Trilithon (Henge)	Green
The Ray of the Priestess	The Flame of Receptivity	Cosmic Lady Ascended Master Isis	60	Lapis Lazuli	The Crescent Moon	Malachite Green
The Spiritual Warrior	The Flame of Mastery	The Master El Morya (King Arthur)	4	Sapphire	Square	Royal Blue
Unconditional Love	The Flame of Cosmic Love	The Archangel Haniel	66	Kunzite	The Heart	Kunzite Pink
Unity	The Flame of Unification	The Master Khutumi (St Francis of Assisi)	5	Yellow Kunzite	Pentagram/Pentacle	Butter Yellow
Wisdom	The Flame of Wisdom	Cosmic Ascended Master Solomon	50	Golden Calcite	A Gold Ring	Gold

A Final Message from the Patrons of the Divine Rays

"Beloved children, children of light,
Your intention to heal others,
your intention to be of service is applauded.
We, The Cherubim, The Great White Brotherhood and Patrons that guard and guide these energies will stand by your side.

We will support you; we will guide you; we will take the love that you shine for your fellow beings and All that there is and expand it for the benefit of your being and the being of your intended.

You are blessed, truly blessed, be not afraid to allow your human form to be the conduit of the healing from the Esoteric Fires.

We will ensure that you are protected in the light of the Divine when you embody this sacred service.

In love we depart but are ever yours, for our role is the support and guidance of mankind, we are ever yours."

The Archangelic Collective The Cherubim
Channelled by Angela Orora Medway-Smith
February 1st 2022

Thank You!

Firstly, I would like to thank my fabulous husband and soul mate for his love and all that he does to support me.

My deepest gratitude goes to these very special souls:

Mary Banks, the Angel Lady of Merlin's Bridge, my dear friend, and teacher who looked after me, under the direction of the Ascended Masters, at her 'Angelic Retreat For All' while I channelled this book.

Kieron Morgan, Brother of Dragons, dear friend and colleague who designed the beautiful illustrations of the Divine Ray symbols, your skill and vision is inspiring.

Edwin Courtenay, whose guidance, generosity and grace continue to inspire me.

Betty Balcombe, my dear friend, teacher, and mentor whose love and humour inspired and encouraged me and built the foundation of my spiritual path.

To the people who have helped this manuscript shine, Annie Williams-Brunt and Michelle Emerson, editor and publisher extraordinaire!

Finally, my gratitude to all those souls who throughout my life have loved, guided and supported me and helped me learn many lessons.

Thank You Thank You Thank You

Bibliography

Alice Bailey - *A Treatise on the Seven Rays* and other titles

Guy Ballard (Godfre Ray King) - *The I AM Discourses* and other titles

Helena Blavatsky - *The Secret Doctrine* and other titles

Edgar Cayce - *The Case for Reincarnation* and other titles

Edwin Courtenay - *Reflections, The Masters Remember, The Archangelic Book of Ritual and Prayer, The Ascended Master Book of Ritual and Prayer, Ascension to Go, Angels to Go, Crystals to Go* and other titles (http://edwincourtenay.co.uk/books.php)

Charles Darwin - *The Power of Movement in Plants*

Shakti Gawain - *Creative Visualisation* and other titles

Judy Hall – *The Crystal Bible (Volumes 1-3)* and other titles

Aurelia Louise Jones - *The Seven Sacred Flames* and other titles

Caitlin Matthews - *The Psychic Protection Handbook: Powerful Protection for Uncertain Times*

Michael Pollan - *The Omnivore's Dilemma* and *The Botany of Desire* https://www.newyorker.com/magazine/2013/12/23/the-intelligent-plant

Philip Permutt -*The Crystal Healer* and other titles

Felicity Warner - *Sacred Oils*

Glossary

Affirmations

The use of commands or instructions that can be used to change the internal programming of the unconscious mind.

Analogous

In biology, an organ that performs a similar function but has a different evolutionary origin.

Angel

A spiritual being superior to humans in power and intelligence, especially one in the lowest rank in the celestial hierarchy.

Archeia

A female archangel, the divine feminine aspect of an archangel.

Archangel

A chief or senior angel in the celestial hierarchy, usually regarded as male.

Ascended Master

Member of the Brotherhood, an enlightened being who has completed their incarnations on Earth and resolved their Karma and chosen to help those who remain on Earth.

Ascension

A process of personal and global evolution.

Ascension Symptoms

Physical side effects felt in different ways by different people as a result of ascension waves.

Aspect

A fragment of either an Ascended Master or Archangelic consciousness which is given individual existence and incarnated on Earth.

Celestial Hierarchy

A traditional hierarchy of angels ranked from lowest to highest into the following nine orders: angels, archangels, principalities, powers, virtues, dominions, thrones, cherubim, and seraphim.

Channel

A medium who receives information and communication, either through trance, clairvoyance, clairaudient or clairsentient from the spirit world and spiritual hierarchy.

Channelling

The act of bringing forth messages from the spiritual worlds either through trance, using 'clair' senses, or telepathic connection.

Cosmic Ascended Masters

A higher version of the ascended master collective containing beings who have moved on from the Ascended Masters to watch over more cosmic occurrences.

Cosmic Ascended Master Collective

Includes the three first souls to be created: Sanat Kumara, the Maitreya and the Maha Cohan.

Etheric Crystal

The etheric imprint of crystal energy without the crystal being physically present.

Invocation

The act or process of petitioning for help or support.

Mala beads

A string of 108 beads traditionally used to count repetitions of mantra.

Mantra

A phrase in English or other language spoken, chanted or sung repetitively to bring changes to the consciousness or reality.

Neurobiology

The study of plant behaviour.

Numerology

The study of the occult significance of numbers.

Occult

Not easily apprehended or understood, hidden from view.

Prayer

An address (such as a petition) to God or a god in word or thought.

Spiritual Protection

A request made to spiritual guides or guardians by way of prayer, ritual, or invocation to protect a space or person before commencing any spiritual work.

Transpersonal Chakras

Chakras that are not part of the physical body (particularly The Stellar Gateway, Soul Star and Earth Star Chakras).

The White Brotherhood or Lodge

Another name for the Ascended Masters.

Other Work by Angela Orora

Angela serves the world under the banner of Cariad Spiritual. Her logo illustrates her belief that we all have the ability to transform and 'Be The Butterfly', soaring and reaching into the flower of life to embrace 'All that there is'.

Life & Soul Alignment Coaching

Angela has supported private clients worldwide for many years. Her unique Life & Soul Alignment Coaching process weaves together traditional life coaching and holistic energy techniques, aligning you to your soul connection and achieving harmony and flow in all areas of mind, body and spirit. Enabling you to soar in all areas of your life and work with grace and flow and a deep connection to source energy.

Ascension Numerology, Channelled Readings, Healing & Spiritual Consultations

Angela offers a range of services to private clients internationally tailored to individual requirements.

Cariad Spiritual Academy offers accredited training in intuitive development, energy healing and spiritual growth, designed to support you to soar, reclaim your sovereign self and 'Be The Butterfly'.

Cariad Spiritual & Rising Phoenix Retreats offer intensive, immersive experiences in beautiful locations worldwide, empowering you with practical tools for spiritual growth in a safe, nurturing space.

Cariad Spiritual Sacred Energy Therapeutics are energetic essential oil blends charged with crystal, sound, and healing energy created to support specific healing issues and spiritual development. A Divine Ray Connection range is also available – see https://www.cariadspiritual.com/shop

Divine Energy International is a charity supporting the spread of energy healing worldwide, a membership organisation and platform for learning and development in different energy healing modalities.

Angela is a founder member and Chair of the Board of Trustees, our vision is: *A World Where Divine Energy Is For All.*

Find out more at www.divineenergyinternational.org

Other Titles

The Book of Many Colours: Awaken Your Soul's Purpose With The Divine Rays (Published November 2021).

Angela is also a featured author in three Amazon Best-Selling Book Series.

The Wellness Universe Complete Guide to Self-Care: 25 Tools for Goddesses (Published by Brave Healer Productions, December 2021).

*Strong Mothers (*Published by Brave Healer Productions, March 2022)

Awaken Your Inner Truth: A Journey of Riches (Published by Motion Media International May 2022).

About the Author

Angela Orora Medway-Smith is a Welsh-born spiritual channel and teacher who has been the conduit for healing for thousands of people worldwide.

She devotes her life to awakening divine souls like you to their potential and believes that we all have the ability to transform, to emerge from the chrysalis of this human life, to 'Be The Butterfly' and SOAR; developing a deep connection to our soul, aligning with our true destiny.

Serving under the banner of Cariad Spiritual, Angela is 'The Practical Mystic' a trusted spiritual channel, teacher and Life & Soul Alignment Coach with a long-standing international client base. She also offers healer training, spiritual development, in person, online and at transformational retreats.

Angela is incredibly blessed to be a direct channel to the Angelic Realm and Ascended Masters, her first book was a channelled book on the Divine Rays called *The Book of Many Colours* which helps people connect to their soul's path through these amazing vibrations which preceded this volume. She is also co-author of three collaborative Amazon Best Selling books.

Angela lives in South Wales with her husband and family.

"...Invoke this Ray to better understand the healing energy of all plants...to select those most fitting with your vibration..."

The Archangel Uriel
Channelled by Angela Orora Medway-Smith
The Book of Many Colours, **April 2021**

Printed in Great Britain
by Amazon